Make the Leap:

From Mom & Pop to Good Enough to Sell

By Genevia Gee Fulbright, CPA

Foreword by
Walter Turek

Edited by
Donald Jay Korn

Cover Design by
Jay Dubard
http://envisual.tripod.com

Copyright © 2005 by Genevia Gee Fulbright, CPA

ISBN 0-7414-2345-6

Published by:

INFINITY
PUBLISHING.COM

1094 New De Haven Street, Suite 100
West Conshohocken, PA 19428-2713
Info@buybooksontheweb.com
www.buybooksontheweb.com
Toll-free (877) BUY BOOK
Local Phone (610) 941-9999
Fax (610) 941-9959

Printed in the United States of America

Printed on Recycled Paper

Published January 2005

To

My family and extended family network

ENDORSEMENTS

"In her latest book in the series, *Make the Leap: From Mom & Pop to Good Enough to Sell*, Genevia Gee Fulbright fills a critical, strategic gap, often overlooked by the small business owner who may myopically focus on growing the enterprise without envisioning a long-term result. By starting with the end in mind, this seasoned entrepreneur and business mentor creates a blueprint that broadens the scope of an owner's thinking and expands the opportunity to bring a business to successful fruition--ensuring that it bears fruit over the long haul, perhaps for generations to come."

- Adrienne Kelly Lumpkin is President of Alternate Access, Inc., a converged communication solution provider. She is President of the National Association of Women Business Owners (NAWBO) in Raleigh, North Carolina.

"*Make the Leap: From Mom & Pop to Good Enough to Sell* is an informative and accurate book, detailing how to assess the value of your business and use this knowledge to grow and/or exit your enterprise."

- Donald R. White, CPA, is Treasurer and Tax Collector, County of Alameda, California

"I will give a copy of this book, *Make the Leap: From Mom & Pop to Good Enough to Sell*, to all of my clients who are ready to make a transition to a new phase in the evolution of their business. It is a much needed map, as they traverse their new road."

- Bert Whitehead, M.B.A., J.D., is a Personal Financial Advisor and Founder of the Alliance of Cambridge Advisors.

"I am convinced this new release, *Make the Leap: from Mom & Pop to Good Enough to Sell*, will eclipse Genevia's earlier successful works in educating those entrepreneurs seeking a practical strategy to maximize their departure options and add value. She uses her boundless knowledge and network of key experts to provide a roadmap to independence."

— John Bernard is a Private Equity Investor in Farmington Hills, Michigan

"*Make the Leap: From Mom & Pop to Good Enough to Sell* answers some of the most critical questions faced by business owners in order to assist you in devising strategies to exit your enterprise. With the help of your professional advisors and by implementing some of the steps outlined in this book, you can preserve wealth and plan for a smoother transition."

— Dennis N. Middleton, CPA, is a tax, business management, and wealth preservation practitioner with offices in Beverly Hills and Oakland, California.

"Having coached thousands of small business and Fortune 1000 CEOs, I find that most are great rainmakers and many are brilliant at operations. Unfortunately, many have not planned for their early retirement or thought about how they will transition their enterprise to the next generation. Management teams should pick up this book, *Make the Leap: From Mom & Pop to Good Enough to Sell*, by Genevia, to give them some helpful food for thought. She has networked with a team of brilliant associates to provide a comprehensive and practical how-to guide for entrepreneurs at this transitional stage in the life of their company."

— Brian "The Sales Doctor" Azar is President of The Sales Catalyst, a corporate coaching and sales consulting firm, and author of *Your Successful Sales Career*

"*Make the Leap: From Mom & Pop to Good Enough to Sell* is an excellent guide for maximizing your company's intrinsic value. It gives you a guide to the decisions that you should make on a daily basis for the best outcome in the long run."

— Connie J. White is Lead Consultant of Geocourt, business advisors to Fortune 1000 companies

"Genevia's new title, *Make the Leap: From Mom & Pop to Good Enough to Sell,* provides an educational approach that is practical, hands-on, and easy to understand. Her insight helps to eliminate the self-doubt and awkward transition that people feel in developing an exit strategy."

— Olalah Njenga is a small business marketing specialist with Make It Write, LLC

"If you want to boost your chances of succeeding more quickly and easily, put *Make the Leap: From Mom & Pop to Good Enough to Sell* at the very top of your reading list. Far better to become well informed and consider your choices BEFORE you take action. This book is an excellent resource and belongs on your personal reference shelf."

— Ruth H. Ledesma, PCC, is a Strategic Thinking Coach and Consultant

Table of Contents

Foreword: Time to Grow

by Walter Turek

Excitement, challenge, exhaustion, exhilaration--these are all feelings experienced throughout an owner's days, weeks, and years in business. Whether its purpose is to serve the best burgers or create the brightest smiles, your business must be profitable. It also must be guided along a path consistent with your vision, your goals, and, ultimately, your exit strategy.

Having worked with thousands of business owners over the years, I've seen many start with a vision and work tirelessly trying to achieve it. However, few of those owners have considered where to go when they're done. Your final goal should not be the success of the business alone; your objectives also should include attracting good buyers for your company, providing a great retirement for yourself, or leaving a worthy legacy to those whom you care about.

How can you get there? You must acknowledge and promote the successes of your employees and your company. You must create an environment conducive to:

* Communicating and encouraging the implementation of your vision

* Providing superior client service

* Making your employees feel valued

* Encouraging those employees to grow personally and professionally, through training and recognition

* Generating profits in order to reward shareholders, employees, and owners

Growing your business from a Mom-and-Pop operation to an enterprise that's good enough to sell requires *at least* these four steps:

1. Know where you are now and how you are currently viewed in the market.

2. Define what you want to be.

3. Study and evaluate the demand for your intended market growth.

4. Start promoting the company with the vision of what it will be.

As you reach each plateau, everyone will be comfortable with the transition to the next level.

At Paychex, we've never limited ourselves to being just a payroll processing company. We have defined ourselves as an employer's administrative company on many fronts. Therefore, by the time we moved aggressively into products and services beyond payroll, such as retirement plans, our employees and the outside world already recognized Paychex as a full service company.

PATIENCE IS PRUDENT

Be patient--you must be disciplined in your growth. Take it in steps. When you reach a plateau, make a business decision and take the next step based on facts, study, test marketing, and experience. As a result, you'll be able to justify your decision and determine how to tweak it, when necessary.

Always stay focused on your next plateau. Once attained, your following plateau objective will be much clearer.

A strategic partnership can be an opportunity for a small business. Ongoing employee training, acquisitions, and strong marketing strategies also can bring efficiencies and fuel growth.

Whatever route you choose, you must be clear on the following: is your ultimate goal to sell the company to outsiders or to leave a legacy, with family or employees buying your interest?

You must remain determined to create and then transform the business into a thriving company. Improving your organization need not be a complex task. Research, training for all involved, and an action plan that's accepted by those responsible for implementation will put you on the path to your goals. Whether your next goal is to improve your business operations, create a dominant market position, or just maintain your successful organization, self-study is the first step.

I hope you enjoy this resource book by Genevia Gee Fulbright, CPA. It will help you to *Make the Leap: From Mom & Pop to Good Enough to Sell.*

Walter Turek

Walter Turek is the Vice President of Sales and Marketing for Paychex, a Fortune 500 company that provides employer administrative services. In his marketing career, spanning more than 25 years, he has coached thousands of sales and marketing professionals as well as entrepreneurs.

Introduction

by Genevia Gee Fulbright, CPA

Many small-business owners start out by concentrating on "making" payroll or by focusing on picking up new clients (even unqualified ones) to generate cash flow. Although day-to-day operations are extremely important for any venture, such an emphasis may restrict long-term opportunities. If an entrepreneur does nothing but address current concerns, who is left to concentrate on the company's strategic plan or succession plan?

Sometimes it can take an entrepreneur a decade or two to come full circle and understand that it takes more than just the ability to pay the bills to make a company successful. Success is not only the amount of money you make but also the enjoyment you derive from the daily operation of your business and the value you add to society.

Successful entrepreneurs understand that building a vibrant company requires that they identify a business focus (a guiding passion), preferred clients, and a brand for the company's products or services. In addition, internal or external professionals must be available to help create formal processes and strategies.

Over the years I've seen successful businesses, big and small. They've all had common traits: leaders with vision, networking savvy, and the ability to attract the right group of professionals to help guide the company.

How can you transform your business into something good enough to sell? That is the question we intend to answer in this book, *Make the Leap: From Mom & Pop to Good Enough to Sell.*

MAKING THE GRADE

As Kenny Lattimore says in one of his popular pieces, "If you could see you through my eyes." If you desire to grow your business into a successful enterprise, you must constantly assess your efforts with a "business report card." Included on this report card should be the answers to such questions as:

* How do others perceive us?

* How are we compared with our peer group?

* Are we making adequate, consistent profits?

* Where do we project sales volume to be in five years?

* Do we have a strategic plan that we use as a guide?

* Do we have a succession plan? An emergency plan?

Always keep in mind that the prospective buyer for your business should be viewed as your company's ultimate customer.

For those of you who are currently in business, say "yes" out loud (don't worry about who's looking) when you can relate to any of the following comments:

* Sometimes I feel I have to lean on clients to collect my receivables.

* Tomorrow I have a light day so I'll work the 10 hours I need to reduce the number of hours I'm required to put in tomorrow.

* I would like to be in the Top 10 percentile in my peer group but I don't know how to get there.

* I'm not sure my revenues are sufficient to justify a salary increase for myself.

* I have great contract proposals but I need more capital so the business can purchase supplies.

* I'm not sure I can borrow all the money I need to expand my business.

* I have a strategic plan, in my head.

* If someone wanted to buy my business today I'm not sure

I'll get what I want.

* I don't know what my business is worth on the open market.

* I'm past the bootstrap stage in my business so I'm ready to grow.

* If I offer more employee benefits I might attract some stronger staff members.

* While I know my target market, attracting more of those customers is my current project.

* I understand my brand and I'm starting to attract stronger clients/customers

* I'm the right leader for my company but I don't have anyone to groom to take over when I am ready to retire.

* I understand that strong internal controls are necessary if I want my company to be successful.

* I have a vision for growth but have not found the time to implement it.

I think Dr. Michael Gerber puts it best in his book, *The E-Myth*. You are not truly an entrepreneur unless the business works for you and not you for the business.

According to Dr. Gerber, some small-business owners subscribe to the entrepreneurial myth: they think owning a business will provide more freedom, flexibility, and independence. However, one must understand that the "price" of freedom sometimes includes long hours and the acquisition of new management skills such as creative strategic thinking, human resources, accounting, and administrative leadership.

The real price for the freedom of business ownership, though, is the risk of not properly setting up your company. If you fail to create the right framework, you always will be putting out fires rather than spending time on the things you really enjoy. Dr. Gerber describes transitioning your business so that it will be an operating unit that works for you, allowing you to have a fulfilling life as well as impressive financial statements.

A WINNING TEAM

For this book, I've pulled together a team of talented contributors. You'll meet numerous successful entrepreneurs, a valuations expert, a finance executive, professors, marketing pros, and others who have shared their practical experiences. The result, I feel, is a book you'll keep around for many years to come. The lessons you learn will help you transition your company into a business that provides exciting opportunities for growth.

This book was written for several reasons. I enjoy sharing practical advice with entrepreneurs and hope to help an unlimited number of entrepreneurs become more successful. If you are at a crossroads with your business, desiring to grow from a small operator to a larger enterprise, you're certain to find some new tools that will help you continue on your path to success.

LEAP OF FAITH

When I embarked on my journey to create a book series, I wanted to provide readers with practical guides that include tips readers could implement immediately, with or without professional help. My goal was to create a consultative, coaching tone that would inspire and empower business owners to take action.

Recently, I appeared as a national seminar panelist for a conference session entitled, "The Road to Wealth: Getting Rich in America." The underlying theme was, "do something." One thing I found early in my career is that I enjoyed collaborating with experts in vital areas. The contributions of such experts to this book provides a reference book that can answer some important questions while prompting readers to seek additional advice, if needed.

The first entry in this book series was, *Make the Leap: Shift from Corporate Worker to Entrepreneur*. With this current title, *Make the Leap: From Mom & Pop to Good Enough to Sell*, the combined experience of all the chapter contributors and advisors exceeds 200 years. Considering what these authors might charge as consultants, the two books provide thousands of dollars worth of advice for less than the cost of a dinner out. I'm confident that both books will generate a good return on your investment; the current entry probably will be one of those books that hang around your office for occasional referencing when a question arises.

Remember, this book is not intended to replace the advice of your personal advisor(s). We encourage all entrepreneurs to engage the services of qualified professionals (CPAs, financial planners, bankers, insurance professionals, attorneys) as valued team members.

WORDS FROM THE WISE

During a recent interview, I asked columnist Michael Shinn, President of Financial Network Investment Corporation, "Why are some business owners successful?"

He responded by saying, "Business owners that succeed have answered two simple questions and backed it up with a third. They have created and articulated a compelling vision of what their business will be in the future. They can see it, taste it and excite others about it."

Next, they have developed a passionate "why" to explain the reason that their business has to exist. The "why" will drive them when the business is at a low point and giving up would be easy to do.

Finally, they have created a "roadmap of how" they will conceive, develop, and grow their business. As Shinn said, "If this sounds like a business plan, it is, but it has to have personality, passion, energy, excitement, and emotion."

Another associate, columnist Jim Verdonik of Daniels, Daniels & Verdonik, PA (listed among the *Best Lawyers in America*), reminds business owners, "When you decide whether to invest in growing your business, determine whether you are likely to get your investment back when you sell the business or by earning increased profits before you sell the business. Approach it like you would decide whether to remodel your house. You usually get more of your investment back on re-sale by remodeling the kitchen than remodeling the basement." That is, "investments" that produce no financial return are really expenses, not investments.

FOOD FOR THOUGHT

In *Make the Leap: From Mom & Pop to Good Enough to Sell*, we'll show you the "kitchen": the key areas on which you should focus so that your small business can improve and become attractive enough to sell. We'll also show you how important it is to seek professional guidance if you're trying to estimate what your company might fetch in the market, what type of individuals to have on your team, and how to attract customers (or acquire them). Follow our advice and you'll create a legacy, regardless of whether you ultimately want to sell your business or if you simply want to get your company in tip-top shape for ongoing operations.

You've made an investment by buying this book. Let us now explore some ways to help you make the leap from a Mom-and-Pop enterprise into something that is good enough to sell.

Preface: Look Beyond Yourself

by Linda L. Poulson, Ph.D., CPA

As a business owner, you must look beyond yourself if you desire your company to become a successful enterprise that is good enough to sell or operate without running out of steam. Of the thousands of entrepreneurs and students I've counseled over the years, I have found that the most successful ones are those who realize early on that building a team that includes professional advisors is critical to the success of the enterprise.

You should take a critical look at your business future when you set up the enterprise, then continue to evaluate your business every year. Who should be on your team?

Your team should consist of those who can help you

* develop your vision;

* create a succession plan;

* form strategic alliances;

* manage cash flow requirements;

* formulate brand awareness and marketing campaigns;

* develop a client niche;

* establish product or service lines;

* secure financing for expansion;

* develop internal staff as well as external advisory boards.

These experts will form a winning team if they enable your business to continue seamlessly once you are ready to relinquish day-to-day responsibilities, or if they bring your company to the point where it can be sold at an attractive price.

There are many other business "musts" that company principals sometimes overlook as they expand its scope.

7

Throughout the life of the business, both independent as well as qualified internal professionals should be relied upon for accounting, tax, and financing needs. Study after study has shown that the greatest challenge for a business owner is the lack of adequate capital, followed by the need for expertise in areas besides dealing with clients.

As Dub Gulley, the Director of DTCC Small Business Center states, "Don't be DOA (dead on arrival) from Day One." Often, a small business will survive (with many sacrifices on the owner's part) for many years, despite the fact that it was really DOA. Doomed at birth, these companies struggled on hopelessly because their owners didn't realize they lacked adequate capital, professional advice, or a management or team that was experienced in taking a business to the next level.

How many times have you wondered why a business that has been in existence for over 20 years would "all of a sudden" close down as soon as the owner dies? Or why another business that has been around for 10 years would prematurely close because of failure to make payroll tax payments to the IRS? Such companies were actually the walking wounded, the living dead, and they inevitably expired.

There are countless stories of business owners who started out with the best of intentions only to succumb to the many pressures of growing a business. Many of these business owners may have had a different outcome had they heeded the old saying, "No man plans to fail, men fail to plan." You must plan your company's future success in order to avoid becoming another failure statistic, even after years in business.

Don't just read this book—become intimately familiar with it. Meditate on its advice. Take the time to utilize the resources of the talented professionals who have contributed. They are all seasoned experts who work with small businesses on a daily basis and can share many good stories with you, the reader.

Begin With the End in Mind
Tuesday Morning:
Who is the Customer?

by Joseph Williams

For some reason I have always pictured selling my company on Tuesday morning. Monday is too busy, Wednesday is hump day, Thursday is almost Friday, and Friday is Friday. Hence, everything I do in business is about Tuesday morning. I am going to take the opportunity to share some thoughts with you about how to make your Tuesday morning as successful as possible.

It is crucial to begin with the end in mind in any endeavor, but particularly as a business owner. That's because the day-to-day grind of running a company is something that some individuals never escape, even after fifty years in business. If you do not plan for the end game, it will never happen. Even if you do not plan to sell your company, planning your life as if you will sell it one day will often result in an immensely better quality of life.

START WITH A CHART

The first step is to draw an organizational chart of what the company will look like on the Monday evening prior to sale. What are the positions and what does each person do? Obviously, this is dependent upon the type of business that you have.

There will be a CEO and President (separate roles if the company is a substantial enterprise), a VP of Sales, VP of Marketing, VP of Operations, a CFO, an HR person, etc. One person may fill most or all of these roles when you begin your company but nonetheless they are roles and they are important.

For example, even in a three-person company there is a person who sells, a person who pays the bills, and a person who

9

produces the product or service. Hopefully, you get the point–an organizational chart and the job descriptions that go along with each position will help you to clearly define where you need to build competencies and eventually hire the absolute best people available.

Constructing an organizational chart before you actually get started in business is what Michael Gerber, the author of *The E Myth*, calls working on your business instead of in your business. This is a key concept, one that's crucial if you ever want to sell your company. Building an organizational chart before actually hiring the individuals to fill those roles is a basic step to begin working on your business.

THE CONTEXT CONCEPT

One of the key barriers to an exit strategy that creates wealth is the inability to understand the difference between selling a company and selling a movement. Most people think about selling a company.

For example, let's say that you have a shoe company that specializes in selling shoes to upper-income women in New York City; Greenwich, Connecticut; and Short Hills, New Jersey. You could look at your business as a shoe retailer that is based in New York, selling X number of shoes to Y customers. That company is worth Z.

However, let's say you think deeply about the context of what you sell. You sell high-end products into one of the most demographically attractive markets in America. You have a database of over 10,000 past customers who are loyal and have high disposable income. Looked at in this way, not only is the company a shoe company but it is also a distribution channel and selling opportunity for any company that wants to reach this marketplace.

I cannot express how important this approach is to achieving a high valuation for your company. For example, the above company may only have $5 million in sales and $400,000 in profits. However, it represents a distribution channel, customer information, and customer access to about $40 million in potential sales of high-end luxury products and $8 million in profits, all within the same customer base. This is called the Context of the Sale, a concept that essentially changes the universe of buyers for your company in a dramatically different way.

EYES ON THE PRIZE

If one were to ask the average business owner, "Who is your customer?" it is extremely unlikely that he or she would consider the eventual buyer of the business to be a customer. However, out of all the sales you make in your lifetime as a business owner, this will be the largest in dollar volume. (If it's not, you have a very serious problem.)

I suggest that you spend a day at the park thinking about the end-of-the-road customer for your business; think about what he or she will find to be important. In fact, as I write this chapter, one thing I am doing is hiring an MBA intern to research exactly that topic. That is how serious my business partner and I take this activity.

Again, this is the largest sale of your life! Spend some time on market research. Determine the desires and wants, patterns of behavior, and customer influencers of your eventual customer. It will pay off!

TIER DROPS

Most industries have multiple levels of competition: international firms, national firms, semi-national firms, regional firms, and Mom-and-Pop operators. In addition, within these tiers there is some differentiating factor that separates the top company from the bottom, besides sales volume. It may be product diversity, delivery time, inventory availability, or professionalism of the sales force.

It is important to understand how your industry is structured in regards to these tiers and in particular where you stand in your industry. At each tier, the valuation changes and the universe of potential buyers expands

Let me provide an example. I am an owner of a staircase company, with four tiers in our industry.

* Tier one is characterized by national players that have huge inventory levels, national distribution partners, multiple levels of professional management, and approximately $40 million to $50 million in sales.

* Tier two has moderate inventory levels but still has national distribution. In addition, professional management can only be found at the top. The size of tier-two companies is about half that of the tier-one firms.

* Tier three is much more regional in scope and focus than either tier one or tier two. There are very few professional managers at this level. Tier-three companies keeps less SKU variety, have regional distribution, and are about half the size of tier-two companies.

* Tier four has extreme fragmentation; the companies are literally Mom-and-Pop outfits. They possess low inventory, almost no professional management talent, and have distribution within a fifty-mile radius.

Your company's value will depend upon where it may be found in this chain. If you are somewhere in the middle of tier three of your industry, it is important to first recognize this fact. Then you must figure out what steps to take in order to change your situation.

Is your customer base slow-paying? Do you sell to a distribution channel that is declining? Are you in a slow-growing region of the country? Do you have to increase your sales by X million to be considered a top-level tier three?

I have found that companies that are in the middle of any tier have a harder time exiting successfully. You must either move to the top of your tier or be content with a lesser valuation.

Finally, there is significant value to getting to the next tier in your business. A fast-growing but small tier-two company often will have a substantially higher valuation than a stodgy, slightly smaller tier-three company. The key is to identify what drives value in your industry and what defines the tiers.

In my business, I am doing everything possible to become one of the largest players in a certain distribution channel. Our goal is to become a tier-one company in a growing and lucrative distribution channel as opposed to a tier-three company in a traditional channel. I expect it will pay off when I eventually decide to exit.

BIGGER + FASTER = BETTER

If you think a small company that is not growing rapidly will deliver a sizable price when you're ready to exit, skip this part of the chapter and continue to use hope as a strategy. However, if you are a realist you should realize that the greatest valuations go to large companies that are growing rapidly. The next level is a small company that has a great growth curve and growth story. Obviously, the lowest valuation will go to a small company with no growth.

Thus, business owners need to grow or die! Meek, no-growth strategies lead to a risky future for your company and very little chance of your selling it for an appreciable price.

Why does size lead to a potential better exit? First, it makes the buyer more comfortable that the company they are buying will endure the change in management. In particular, a middle management team adds to this comfort.

Second, if financing is necessary for the purchase, investors and banks are much more comfortable with a larger company. Finally, a larger company will attract experts to help sell the business. These experts, investment bankers or high-quality business brokers, will build the type of demand for a sizable company that is only a dream for many small businesses.

GOOD PEOPLE, GOOD NEWS

A very close friend of mine tells me that marriage is the only real decision that matters in life. One can agree or disagree with this opinion.

In business, my opinion is that two things matter: first, having good people on the team; and second, please refer to the first item mentioned.

As you are building your company for an eventual exit, it is crucial to realize that all that the eventual customer will buy is a group of people who are implementing a system. That is all that is for sale: the people and systems that are in place as well as their ability to generate wealth for the new owner.

To assemble a team of high-quality people, you must change your focus regarding personnel. First, you will need to implement a rigorous selection process that evaluates character, fit, skills, and growth potential, among other factors. Second, you will have to develop a philosophy of, 'When in doubt about a hire, wait.' Don't rush to hire someone who's not an obvious choice.

Third (and this is a hard one), you will have to turn down highly-skilled people who are short-term, fix-it types. Instead, select people for the long-term. Such applicants may have fewer specific skills but they'll offer character, work ethic, and the attitude to improve the team, along with the ability to uplift the entire organization.

STRATEGY SESSION

It is not a mistake that the strategy portion of this chapter comes after people. As expressed in the book, *Good to Great*, by Jim Collins, I fundamentally believe and have learned from experience that getting the right people is more important than strategy. The right people will literally point you in the direction of the right strategy.

In regards to strategies for companies, particularly for small companies, I think the following steps are key (again assuming that the right people are on board):

One, recognize the strengths of your competitors. What customers will they fight tooth and nail not to lose?

Two, recognize that going after their prime customers may trigger a vicious response. Therefore, it may be better to pursue a market niche that competitors will not or cannot enter.

Three, figure out what competitive advantage you have or what competitive advantage you could create.

Four, think about what you would enjoy and what would be fun.

Eventually, a viable strategy will evolve from talking to customers, suppliers, competitors, and, most importantly, by listening to your employees.

SALES UP, COSTS DOWN

Every business needs to be able to articulate a description of its key customer. This is vital: if you design your business around that customer, the eventual buyer of your company is not only buying your company's sales but also the infrastructure to service that key customer.

In my business, for example, if you have infrastructure to service builders with staircase parts it is likely that you could sell flooring products through the same distribution channel. If your business is designed to service a certain customer, all companies that service that same customer will have some interest in your company.

Remember, money is only made if a sale takes place and most acquisitions are based on either revenue or cost synergies. What does this mean? A buyer, particularly another company, will look for ways that it can either add to its revenue or reduce its costs by acquiring your company. Those are the main reasons for one company to buy another.

Cost synergies might include volume purchasing, reducing overhead, integrating IT and back office functions, and various other methods, depending on the business. Cost synergies are fine but revenue synergies tend to lead to higher valuations. That's especially true if the new buyer sees the potential for exceptional revenue increases.

Designing your business around the key customer is a way to ensure that the potential buyer is able to realize these synergies. Selling such synergies is an effective way to enhance your wealth at the time your company changes hands.

CHOOSING CHANNELS

In most businesses there are various ways to get your product to market. It could be through manufacturers' reps, wholesale outlets, retail outlets, or direct to the end customer. Each business is unique and I cannot say what channel is best. However, I know that in most businesses there are trends either towards indirect distribution through middlemen or direct distribution, which would service the end customer. In many industries there has been a shift toward direct distribution.

The key is to notice the trends in your business and be aware of them. It is important to study the distribution channels in regards to your capacity and ability to service the channel effectively. If your resources match a particular channel better than others, consider being Number One in that channel, as long as it is relatively attractive.

Some issues to consider in choosing channels are the level of inventory and working capital that a given channel will require, the cash conversion cycle of a channel, its growth rates, the competition, and, of course, your ability to service the channel effectively. Recognizing the channel issue and making a decision based on exit valuation is a key step that a lot of companies do not understand.

BY THE BOOK

Manuals, methods, employee handbooks, and turnkey systems add value to your company. Just as a homeowner who has taken care of his or her landscaping can expect more interest from home buyers, a business that has systems and procedures in place is more likely to be buyer-friendly.

Through my work in business acquisitions, I have run into companies that keep horrible records, seem to under-report income, and have inventory that is not accounted for on their balance sheets. However, they want to add such income and inventory to their valuation.

This is an extremely tough sell to a buyer. In addition, a company that does not have proper systems may have legal liability that may make it un-saleable. For example, the lack of an employee handbook could lead to a lawsuit on an issue that could have been settled if proper procedures and policies had been in place.

LOOKING OUT FOR NUMBER TWO

If you are everything to your business, you simply cannot sell it. It is important that approximately two to three years prior to selling your company you begin to develop a person that fills a "General Manager" role.

This person will assure the buyer that all the knowledge does not reside in your head. Often, even if this person is not an absolute rock star it will increase your valuation because the buyer will feel comfortable that he will have someone to work with if you the owner are not motivated after the sale of the business.

Many a buyer has overpaid for a company because a General Manager was in place. Very few small companies take this step.

ABOUT FACE

As important as marketing literature is to secure customers, it is also important to present a professional image to the buyer. Cheap marketing literature tells a buyer that the company is unprofessional. A sophisticated buyer may discount the price by what he or she feels he will have to spend after purchase in marketing to match what the competition is offering.

Good marketing literature can make a company appear larger than it really is. This image of being a larger company may interest your competitors or indirect competitors in purchasing your professionally-run organization.

On the other hand, poor marketing literature is often a symbol of being in the lower tiers of your industry. Simply upgrading the quality of your marketing material may push you above the bottom rung of your industry and increase your value in buyers' eyes.

COURTING CUSTOMERS

Every business owner loves repeat customers because they have a relatively low acquisition cost, compared with their lifetime revenue. In addition, orders from repeat customers are somewhat predictable, which helps a business owner forecast demand for various products or services.

Essentially, repeat business reduces the risk of operating a business and provides a customer base from which to grow. Because such repeat customers are valuable to a purchaser of the business, you should make every effort to attract and retain them. Document the percentage of your sales that are repeat business, recurring revenues, or contract-based.

On the other hand, customer concentration is an issue that can reduce valuation. Suppose, for example, that company A has $10 million in annual sales but $4 million comes from one customer. Company B also has $10 million in sales but its largest customer only accounts for $1 million in revenues. If you were the buyer, which business would be more attractive?

Most buyers would prefer B, with lower customer concentration, because there is less risk in such a business.

Therefore, as a business owner it is important for you to reduce customer concentration as much as possible, not just for a higher selling price but also to reduce the risk of operating your company.

SELL YOURSELF

The final step to a happy exit is becoming known in your industry. You'll find it worthwhile to speak at industry associations and trade shows; you might write a column in an industry periodical. This can help you, and effectively your company, become known as a leader in a given space.

Tier-four or tier-three companies do not get involved in these activities. When you make a name for yourself, you'll find that it's a great way to differentiate yourself, raise the visibility of your company, and meet your potential buyer.

SUMMARY

I hope this chapter has helped you think about Tuesday morning, a special day in any business owner's life. Even if you do not want to sell, thinking of your company with the idea that perhaps you might sell will provide a rational underpinning for key business decisions and improve the quality of your life.

Good luck as you prepare for Tuesday morning!

Recommended Books

Good to Great, by Jim Collins

The E-Myth Revisited, by Michael Gerber

The Art of M&A Structuring: Techniques for Mitigating Financial, Tax & Legal Risk, by Alexandra Reed Lajoux and H. Peter Nesvold

Who Should Be At The Top?

by Paul Rasmussen

The question of "Who should be at the top?" is one that confronts countries, organizations, and companies, large or small, from time to time. It may be a question that is facing you right now.

Your answer to this question might be, "It's my company, so I should be on top." If you are satisfied with where your company is today and you want to keep it that way, then that may be the right answer.

However, if you aspire to build your company beyond what it is today for the purpose of selling it, or to create a viable and sustaining legacy, other questions might arise. When you ask, "Who should be at the top to take this company where I want it to go?" the answer may be very different.

Several additional questions that you might consider are: Where am I? What is my goal? How am I going to get there? What is standing in my way? What am I missing? What might I have to give up to get to where we want to go? Those are all good questions, so I'll address them. Let's assume that you started your company and you own all of it, or a majority interest. It's your baby, your creation, and you got it to where it is today. You have employees, and they probably work hard, but you built it.

As your company has expanded and grown, you've encountered new challenges that have required you to learn new skills. Now you have a goal that requires you to take the company to another level. How are you going to acquire the abilities and knowledge to reach that next level and accomplish your goal?

If you had an unlimited amount of time, boundless energy, as well as the ability to learn and master everything, there would be no problem. You could take the time, expend the energy, and master all that may be required to reach your goal.

Few of us have unlimited time or boundless energy, though, so we have to look at other ways to reach our goals. You might have to look outside of the company for someone who has the skills, knowledge, experience, and possibly the contacts that will help your company continue its growth. Bringing in outside help is not uncommon.

LESSONS IN LEADERSHIP

Before you get nervous about making a change at the top consider the leadership of an organization. A good leader is not necessarily the right leader for all times. What you want is the right leader at the right time.

As an organization and its environment evolves, leadership changes are sometimes necessary. Companies have needs that require different talents at different times. People acquire talents and knowledge and comfort levels that make them best suited to lead at particular times in a company's development.

My personal experience is that I have been best suited to lead a company from an early stage through its growth to an acquisition or an initial public offering. Of the companies that I have started, and those where I was brought in to lead, I was never the initial founder or chief technologist. What I brought to the game was the ability to grow the company and reach a goal: a successful exit.

At this point, you may be asking yourself some difficult questions: If I were to hire someone to lead or manage my company, what is this going to cost? What am I going to give up? Am I going to lose control of my business? Am I going to lose the ownership of my business?

Those are difficult questions, but there are answers. Yes, it is going to cost you something, and you are going to have to give something up. But, if you do it right, you will lose neither control nor ownership of your business. What you are doing is "buying" talent, knowledge, experience and credentials.

GIVE AND GET

Just as you should do when contemplating any major purchase, when you decide to hire outside leadership you must understand how much value you anticipate getting in return for what you'll pay. This "price" may have several parts, such as salary, bonuses, stock, or stock options. What you would be giving up is some (possibly all) of the day-to-day management or operational control, *not ownership control*.

Remember that the structure of a company reflects its ownership, its direction, and where the company is, at a particular point in time. Structure also affects the type of leader you would be able to attract and how he or she would be compensated.

For example, if your company is a sole proprietorship, you own it and you're in charge. If you were to bring someone in to lead or manage the company, he or she would be an employee, without any ownership interest. In this situation, you probably would use salary and incentive-based bonuses to attract this person.

However, salary and bonuses alone may not be enough of a lure to attract the person who can help you accomplish your goals. Further, if your company is a sole proprietorship and you consider using ownership as an incentive, your company's structure will have to be changed to accommodate this. In these circumstances, be sure to consult with your attorney and your CPA before changing your company structure in order to use company ownership as a recruiting tool.

When you're seeking to bring a new leader on board, the culture of your company is just as important as the structure of your company. By culture, I mean the philosophy and social interaction that exist within your company. To a large extent the tone of your company, at least "the tone at the top," is set by you in your social interaction with employees.

The company's culture also will be influenced by the interaction among employees and possibly by your relationships with customers and with the community where you operate. If you make the decision to bring in someone from the outside to lead your company, some modifications of the tone at the top will be needed.

One change to consider is the way in which you think of the business. Going forward, I will refer to "the" company, not "your" company. This is a small change in tone but one that will have to be made with the advent of a new leader.

On a larger scale, the philosophy and culture that you have created are of greater importance. If these are successful, then you don't want to change them. They are real strengths of the company and you don't want them weakened by bringing in someone who might damage or adversely affect them. Conversely, if there are weak points in the philosophy or the social interaction among management, employees, customers, and the community at large, then the addition of a person with skills in this area would be beneficial if not necessary in attaining your goals.

LOOK BEFORE LEAPING

In hiring a new leader, you are in effect hiring your replacement. This new person is going to be in charge, managing the company on a day-to-day basis. What should you look for in such a person? How will you find someone? How will you make the transition palatable for all concerned? There is much to consider and much to plan.

When you think about the type of person whom you're looking for, it is of the utmost importance that this person be someone that you can trust and work with. You are going to be entrusting him or her not only with the responsibility of managing the company, but also with your future wealth and security, to some degree.

Honesty and morals are critical; you have to be able to trust this person. In the course of business, it is not only normal but expected that an in-depth background check be done on any candidate before you offer a key position. There is a cost to having a background check done professionally but it is money well-spent.

Skipping a thorough evaluation can be even more costly. There are many stories about companies, both private and public, that hired top managers whose misstated credentials were not discovered because of an incomplete (or nonexistent) background check. When the truth came out, the credibility of the owners, the board of directors, and the investors was damaged as well as the company's image in the marketplace. Don't let this happen to you or the company; get the best background check that money can buy.

PERSONALITY'S A PLUS

After character, the second most important issue to be addressed would be the candidate's "people skills." The leader the company needs will have the ability to interact with employees, customers, suppliers, owners, investors, and service providers such as the company's banker, lawyer, and auditor. Even if the newcomer's style differs from yours, it is critical that the tone of the company be maintained by the new leader, who may be representing the company more than you do, going forward.

Similarly, your ability to interact with the new leader, in public and private, will be critical. There must be a mutual respect from the beginning, a respect that grows as time goes on. I'm not suggesting that you'll become the best of friends but, if that should happen, it would a nice side benefit. What I am suggesting is that a genuine respect should develop concerning each others' abilities, ideas, and philosophies concerning the business as well as the goals that have been set.

Potential candidates may be found in various places. Individuals whom you know from your own industry may be sought; you also may get referrals from acquaintances or use professional recruiters. Occasionally, an individual may recognize the potential of the company and approach you directly. In fact, I have done this twice myself.

WIN-WIN

The first time, a software company named TGV, Inc., was started by two extremely competent programmers who had no business experience whatsoever. During our initial meetings, I proposed a plan to build the company to a point where we could either be acquired or do an initial public offering within four years. My plan succeeded in scaring them off–they didn't hire me.

However, nine months later those programmers contacted me and proposed that I work with them as a consultant for three or four months, in order to see how things would work out. I signed on as COO. Within four years, the company had its initial public offering and one year later the company was acquired by Cisco Systems.

In my second such experience, I approached the founder of an even smaller company, Beame & Whiteside Software, Inc. I was hired as the CEO and had a similar plan, but the time frame turned out to be much shorter. In its first year of business, the company did a little over $5 million in revenue, with a projection of about $9 million in revenue for the second year. Two months into the second year of business, the company was acquired by a publicly-traded Canadian software company, Hummingbird Communications, Ltd.

In both of these endeavors, the company founders and I developed relationships of mutual respect and understanding. The individual roles and responsibilities were clearly understood; each of us knew what the objectives were. We had a "shared vision" of what the culture of the company was to be as well as agreement about the message that we wanted to send out to the marketplace.

MORE MAY NOT BE MERRIER

Our focus so far has been on companies owned or controlled by individuals. Frequently, even small companies have more than one owner or outside investors with a say in the goals and the direction of the company. In such an environment, the principal stakeholders or owners must have a shared vision of the company's goals and objectives.

Moreover, there must be group agreement on the title, roles, responsibilities, and incentive package that are given to the new leader. Having been on both sides of a group process, I can assure you that it is longer, more strenuous, and more emotional than one that involves only a sole proprietor. When there is a group, there must be group agreement; with any group there are different opinions, agendas, egos, biases, and occasionally a reluctance to make a decision or commitment.

If you are the individual tasked with the responsibility of finding and hiring a new leader, you have to be the one to set the goals and establish the time line. It will be up to you to define what the company is looking for and what it wants to accomplish. You'll have to establish the roles and responsibilities, the incentive package, and the measurements used to determine whether goals have been attained. That's certainly not an easy task, considering that you will have to keep the group focused and in compliance with the time line.

PAY FOR PERFORMANCE

On several occasions I have been hired by the directors of private and public companies. As a result, I have experienced how the hiring process can drag on, usually because of a reluctance to make a decision. Commonly, the directors fear they're paying too much or that they won't get the desired results.

One way to put those fears to rest is by proposing that the new leader receive a smaller salary but a larger bonus or stock reward if the goals and objectives are met. The key to this solution is that the goals and objectives must be mutually agreed upon, realistic, measurable, and achievable within a reasonable period of time.

I've been on the other side of the process, too, as an initial investor in a high-tech startup, Innosoft International, Inc. In that case, the goal was to hire a CEO to manage and build the company while being able to work with the three founders, who were extremely competent programmers and academicians. During this process, one of the founders was reluctance to make any commitment.

As the person responsible for the hiring process, I forced

the issue by saying that if we could not reach full agreement, I would stop the process and the company would continue on as it was. The founders realized that if a decision was not made, the goals and objectives of the company would be delayed or possibly never accomplished. Consequently, full agreement was reached, the process continued, and a CEO was hired. Several years later the goal of the company was achieved when the company was acquired by Sun Microsystems.

BOUNCING BACK

Another company, where I became involved as an initial investor, SciQuest, Inc., started out as a "dot-com". SciQuest was heavily funded, had an initial public offering, and did not fare well when the dot-com bubble burst. The company was managed by its founders, who had industry experience in their targeted market. Within two years it had become apparent to the board of directors that a change at the top was needed.

While the search was underway for a new CEO, I was contacted by a friend who was an experienced executive and whose own company had been acquired by a publicly-traded company. He expressed his interest in SciQuest and asked if he could use me as a reference. Being acquainted with the chairman of the board and several board members, I agreed.

He was subsequently hired and, with the support of the company's board, developed a plan to change the direction of the company. SciQuest reduced its size, sold off nonessential operations, and focused on its core business during the next two years. At that point, the company's size and position were such that it became apparent it would be best if it were no longer publicly-traded.

At the current time, the process is underway to take SciQuest private. All of this has been accomplished because (1) the right person was hired at the right time; (2) clearly understood goals and objectives were developed, with realistic time frames; and (3) the new CEO and the incumbent officers established mutual respect and support.

SUMMARY

Bringing someone into a company to move it to the next level is neither abnormal nor unusual. The driving force behind such a decision is the realization that something else is needed to reach the company's goals. In order for new leadership to succeed, the parties involved must define realistic goals and objectives that are measurable and achievable within a reasonable time frame.

The ideal candidate will be honest, have the necessary skills as well as experience, and possess the contacts required to reach the company's goals. Finding such an applicant is challenging but not impossible.

To wind up with a qualified new leader, the company must take the time to select a candidate who can be objective, embrace and enhance the company's culture, and establish mutual respect with the existing owner. Such an applicant also should get along with the company's directors, investors, employees, customers, and any other key individuals who may affect the firm's future.

Finding such a leader can be challenging but the challenge can be lessened though the use of professional executive recruiters, industry contacts, and professional service providers such as lawyers or auditors. Whatever sources you use for this process, make sure you have a thorough background check performed.

Finally, in order for this undertaking to be successful, the new leader must have the support of the company, it owners, and its directors. The goals, objectives, and responsibilities must be clear, completely understood, and mutually agreed upon. This applies to the compensation package as well.

My experience has been that going though this process has been of great benefit to a company. It requires a fresh look at the company's current position and a reassessment of its future, resulting in a clearer understanding of where you want the business to go.

Best of luck, and don't forget the background check.

Recommended Books

The Right CEO: Straight Talk About Making Tough CEO Selection Decisions, by Frederick W. Wackerle

Effective Succession Planning: Ensuring Leadership Continuity and Building Talent from Within, by William J. Rothwell

Searching for a Corporate Savior, by Rakesh Khurana

The Leadership Pipeline, by Ram Charan

Operations Can Hold Your Company Together

by Deborah Cowan, CPA

Fierce competition, market volatility, and pressure to sustain revenue as well as profit growth have forced companies to increase their focus on the major drivers of their business, over much longer time frames. Today, it is not uncommon for top executives to have a game plan for the company that covers the next five to ten years.

These plans tend to be strategic. That is, they usually are prepared with a top-down approach, focusing on key business metrics and indicators, with little reliance on details. While details may be lacking, the strategy and nature of the plan must be specific enough that managers can understand it, can embrace it, and can link it to their daily operations as well as to their individual and unit objectives.

At a minimum, key management and vital players should be able to ascertain:

(1) where the company's industry is headed;

(2) what business or lines of business the company will be in;

(3) major product assumptions;

(4) the company's competitive position; and

(5) any relevant regulatory matters.

The plan should be accompanied by a financial model that addresses critical company financial metrics, which might include revenue growth, market share, profitability, cash flow, and stock price.

Ideally, a company's plan will not be static, like an annual operating budget. Instead, it should be fluid and subject to change.

Strategic plans should be reassessed on an ongoing basis and updated for major changes in assumptions, in order to keep the company headed in the desired direction.

BOTTOM-LINE BUDGETING

Well-developed plans, however, are of no value unless they are driven down into company operations. An annual operating budget is the tool most commonly used to link strategic planning with daily operations.

A detailed budget can tie the daily operations of each unit to the overall corporate strategy. Such a budget provides the detailed road map to the company's near-term time horizon (typically one to three years) while showing the management team how to reach longer-term, strategic goals. Budgets not only help managers better understand how their unit goals contribute to corporate strategy, they also can coordinate interaction between business units. When budgets identify risks and opportunities, they ultimately will result in better performance.

Budgets also serve as a formal, systematic process to allocate a company's finite resources. Often, there are many competing needs for a company's resources, be they financial resources, such as development or operating expense; physical resources, such as equipment or facilities; or human resources, such as new business developers or sales representatives. Budgets help companies fairly and equitably resolve these competing necessities, enabling management to set priorities and allocate the company's investments in those areas that best support its key strategies.

In addition to communicating goals, supporting strategy, and allocating resources, budgets also serve as a financial control tool. Budgets often establish targets for key financial components of a company's strategy, such as market share, revenue growth, expenses, profit, and cash flow. More comprehensive budgets also will establish non-financial targets, such as customer satisfaction measures, and operational metrics such as faster customer response times.

BUILDING A BUDGET

Can a budget really serve all the above purposes? Yes, if done properly. Here's a simple process for developing a budget:

Create a calendar. The budget process should start with a calendar that lists key participants for specific tasks such as kick-off, preparation, review, approval, and distribution. Time frames and deadlines for each step also should be delineated.

Determine specific programs. In keeping with company strategy, current, new, and obsolete programs should be evaluated for resource allocations, reductions, or eliminations.

Prepare the budget. This involves budgeting specific elements for the upcoming fiscal year or years, such as revenue, expense, profit, head count, and capital. For consistency, and for the purpose of meeting expectations, the individual who is designated as "owner" of the budget process (usually the chief financial officer) should establish financial targets and develop a format. Moreover, the CFO should issue guidance and assumptions prior to the start of budget preparation.

In preparing budgets, many companies are shifting away from traditional spreadsheet tools, which are manually intensive, time consuming, prone to error, and, most important, not integrated with other financial planning or reporting systems. To reduce the time required for producing budgets, these companies are now using web-based budgeting software tools and multi-dimensional data warehouse capabilities to quickly collect, revise, analyze, and consolidate needed budget information.

Analyze and consolidate. Individually prepared budgets should be submitted to the budget owner, who can evaluate and analyze the submission for accuracy, reasonableness, adherence to guidelines, and impact on resources. The budget is then assembled for review by executive management.

Review the budget. Here, executive management should review the budget in detail, propose revisions, and approve resource allocation decisions. Then a budget document can be assembled for board approval.

Obtain board approval. After modifications from the review are made, executive management should submit a detailed budget document to the company's board of directors, for review and approval.

Communicate the approved budget. The approved budget should then be communicated and distributed to unit managers prior to the start of the fiscal year so that they can resolve any questions and use the budget to get off to a fast start.

Track and monitor progress. Unexpected business and competitive conditions are bound to develop. At least monthly, unit managers should monitor actual-to-budget variances, determine causes, and develop corrective action plans as necessary.

FORECASTS, NOT PREDICTIONS

Once deployed, simply tracking and monitoring budget variances are not enough to effectively manage company operations. In order to make more informed decisions, companies must anticipate near-term results by preparing a forecast.

Forecasting involves predicting a company's near-term results, typically for two or three quarters. However, because forecasting is more inclusive than predicting, it facilitates improved and informed decision-making.

Accurate forecasts aid companies in making decisions in critical areas such as purchasing, production, inventory management, resource deployment, logistics, and distribution. Companies not only use forecasts to pro-actively manage their business, but those that are publicly held also use them to provide authoritative market and investor guidance.

Approaches to forecasting are varied yet those companies that have an effective forecasting process tend to follow a common approach:

Designate a forecast "owner." To ensure that forecasts are formal, periodic, and timely, companies should assign responsibility for this task to a group that has the required time, resources, and skills. Forecast owners should involve participants from relevant departments in order to capture all relevant data and to establish credibility for the forecast throughout the organization.

Create one demand forecast. Both sales and production rely heavily on a demand forecast for their respective activities. Without a single, integrated demand forecast, these two separate yet related units will develop demand forecasts to meet their respective planning needs that not only duplicate efforts, but are likely to reach very different conclusions.

While inventory is often the common link between sales and production, both groups view inventory levels quite differently. Sales always wants to meet customer demands for products, while manufacturing wants stable production plans, without over-stocked inventory levels. Obtaining a buy-in from both groups on a single picture of demand not only will result in more complete information, it will help reconcile the often conflicting goals between sales and production.

Have units prepare forecasts. Credible, reliable forecasts start with input from unit managers. They are closer to the competitive and market conditions for their aspect of the business so they are the ones best positioned to provide insight into future expectations. By requiring unit managers to prepare forecasts, the company will reduce the chance that key assumptions or dependencies are being overlooked. Finally, involving unit managers also ensures they buy into the forecast because they can be held accountable if their forecasts turn out to be inaccurate.

Have finance analyze and consolidate forecasts. A company's finance department or executive should assume responsibility for analysis and consolidation of the individual units' forecast submissions. Finance personnel should evaluate forecast submissions for accuracy, adherence to guidelines, reasonableness, and probability of execution.

When analyzing forecasts, consideration should be given

to both internal and external factors, including general and local economic conditions, competitive factors, historical and recent trends, pricing levels, shipments, orders on hand or contract backlog, significant account performance, special promotions, and new or withdrawn offerings. After outlining the forecast's risk and opportunities, finance personnel should then review the forecast with executive management, in order to gain further insight into information that might not be generally available but may impact the forecast.

Monitor forecast accuracy. In order to produce more accurate and reliable forecasts, companies must monitor their forecasts for changing assumptions. Any biases that may be contributing to missed forecasts should be identified. Variables impacting the forecast should be regularly assessed and factored into an updated forecast. Furthermore, companies should track their forecast accuracy and investigate the reasons for missed forecasts. Such follow-up will help to identify and eliminate any biases or flaws from future forecasts as well as establish a general range of reliability.

While many companies follow some or all of the above approaches to forecasting, they differ in exactly how their forecasts are assembled. Specifically, forecasts may vary as to what time frame they cover, how frequently they're prepared, and what level of detail they include.

Short-term forecasts are more accurate yet long-term forecasts give way to future unforeseen conditions that may impact results. Hence, many companies are forecasting beyond the current or near-term periods–they are adopting a rolling-quarter forecast of several months or quarters that reach far into the next fiscal year.

Compiling forecasts can be time consuming and may take away time from operating a business. Thus, companies should focus on delivering accurate and reliable initial forecasts, in order to reduce the frequency of subsequent forecasts or forecast revisions.

Given the necessity of preparing forecasts quickly and

ensuring that those forecasts contain the information essential to gauge expected results, companies are shifting to forecasts that are prepared with less and less detail. Although most companies are not quite adopting a total top-down approach, as they are in the planning stage, many organizations are moving away from preparing forecasts with the same bottom-up detail used to prepare operating budgets.

PAYOFF IN PERFORMANCE

"How did they do?" "What should their bonus be?" These are often the questions that are asked when evaluating performance. The emphasis is on whether or not objectives were really obtained.

Before reaching this point, though, companies should have aligned individual performance objectives to the strategic objectives of the company. If the company's strategy includes revenue growth or market share, for example, these goals should be cascaded down to unit managers for their specific markets or products. Effectively linking the company's strategic goals to individual performance objectives will motivate managers to achieve those goals, thus improving the likelihood the company will achieve its objectives or at least come closer to doing so.

The elements that companies consider when gauging performance have changed drastically, in that many have shifted away from measuring only financial results. Financial results are nothing more than an internal lagging historical indicator of performance.

Today, the intensely competitive and volatile marketplace has put more focus on external and leading indicators. The use of a balanced scorecard that encompasses not only financial measures, but also other leading predictive and internal operational measures, is increasingly popular.

A common balanced scorecard is one that triangulates internal and external financial metrics with operational as well as customer measures.

Financial measures may include such goals as revenue

growth, cash flow, productivity, and profitability.

Customer-focused goals may include market share or some other measure of customer satisfaction. In the broadcast industry, for example, Arbitron or Nielsen share ratings are often used to measure customer receptiveness.

Operational goals tend to be business-process related. Producing more defect-free products or hiring a targeted number of sales representatives are examples of operational goals. With the accelerated reporting deadlines recently imposed by the Securities and Exchange Commission, many public companies have undertaken the operational goal of streamlining their reporting process, which includes shortening the process of closing financial statements to a matter of days instead of weeks.

Tying performance pay to meeting various types of goals can help to ensure that your company meets your long-term goal: growing into an enterprise that offers substantial value to would-be buyers.

SUMMARY

All companies should implement a formal budgeting and forecasting process to measure and plan growth. Both long-term and short-term financial goals are critical if you plan to maintain the growth of your company.

Recommended Books

Balanced Scorecard Step-by-Step Maximizing Performance and Maintaining Results, by Paul R. Niven

Budgeting: Technology, Trends, Software Selection, and Implementation, by Nils H. Rasmussen, Christopher J. Eichorn

Dominate Your Industry:
Combine Brilliant Branding With
Masterful Marketing

by Genevia Gee Fulbright, CPA

You may be skeptical when you hear that a small company is working on defining its brand. In fact, you may ask why would a small business bother with this exercise when there are so many operating issues to consider: project management, staff supervision, product development, and competitive positioning, just to name a few.

Such skepticism, though, is unwarranted. Every company, no matter how big or small, should have a marketing plan. Included in this plan, moreover, should be a strategy to increase brand awareness through an organized public relations campaign.

Those companies that invest in brand awareness usually are in a comfortable negotiating position when it comes time to sell the enterprise. Every successful business owner can describe a typical customer and a key market segment. Once a business owner has defined his or her market, effective marketing strategies can be implemented.

According to public relations and copywriting consultant Valerie K. Fields, President and CEO of V. K. Fields & Co., "Your internal or external marketing professionals should handle the external communications to help articulate who the company is to the rest of the world. Public relations is both an art and a science that requires skill and networking savvy as well as relationships in business, media, and political realms."

Fields asserts that the public's perception of your company inevitably becomes reality. "In such a competitive marketplace," she explains, "presenting the right image may be the determining factor that seals the deal or sways the public's perception in your favor. This momentum can lead to additional clients coming on board or a potential business suitor signing the purchase documents."

THE MANY FACES OF MARKETING

There are numerous definitions of the term marketing as it relates to the business environment. I have found three that I like:

* The American Marketing Association's definition: The process of planning and executing the conception, pricing, promotion, and distribution of ideas, goods, and services to create exchanges that satisfy individual and organizational objectives.

* Merriam-Webster's dictionary definitions: 1: the process or technique of promoting, selling, and distributing a product or service; 2: an aggregate of functions involved in moving goods from producer to consumer.

* Jeffrey J. Fox's definition (he is the author of *How to Become a Rainmaker* and *How to Become a Marketing Superstar*): The profitable identification, attraction, getting, and keeping of good "okay" customers.

BRAND BREAKTHROUGH

What does this have to do with the small business that you're trying to grow, sell or get organized? Part of your marketing plan should include goals for defining your company "brand," which is the manner in which you want others to view your product or service. What does your company stands for? Do you want your product or service to be viewed as being far superior, best priced, reasonably priced, sturdy, high quality, value priced? The goal is to define your brand to attract loyal, qualified customers who value your goods or services and come back for more.

At Fulbright & Fulbright, we started developing successful client attraction methods after we defined our target market. One of the first questions we ask our prospective clients is, "Are you ready for our level of service?" We then immediately proceed to explain how to do business with us, specify the various levels of service available, and describe our ideal client.

We started this process many years ago because we found that failing to qualify or define your brand properly limits your ability to attract compatible prospects. At the end of the day, you always want to be able to reconcile the wants, needs, and desires of your clients with the services or products you deliver.

Marketing experts generally agree that a company must make an effort to:

* Define itself (company products and services)
* Identify the desired target clientele and market segment
* Devise and implement the marketing plan
* Measure effectiveness of strategies
* Continue to reinvent itself as a company

Having a well-implemented marketing plan will add to the company's purchase price because the new owner or leader will not have to create a plan from scratch.

DON'T BE TONE DEAF

Besides normal marketing policies, such as the company's public relations efforts and generating senior management exposure in the media, budgets are required for marketing expenses. An inclusive marketing plan should be "in writing," and visited at least annually.

As part of this plan, you should devise a tone or voice that will carry through advertisements, public relations, and marketing communications with internal as well as external consumers. Your internal team members as well as the market being served should find your marketing pieces attractive; you need buy-in from all involved.

There is nothing worse, for your company's well-being, than having a prospective client talk to a management team member at an outside function and not hearing them about the company's products or services. Such discussions can provide a perfect opportunity to promote your company or at least show pride in the goods or services it produces.

As a child, do you remember playing word association games? There are numerous Web sites that contain an interactive associative thesaurus. Such a reference tool is sometimes known as a psycholinguistic database, such as the Edinburgh Associative Thesaurus (referred to as EAT). Some samples of this process, as part of your branding exercise, include the following:

When you hear:	What do you think of?
Hamburger	McDonald's
Premium coffee	Folgers or possibly Starbucks
Bottled water	Perrier (back in the 70s), now possibly Evian
Dr. Phil	Oprah
Mark Victor Hansen	*Chicken Soup for the Soul*
Basketball	Michael Jordan or possibly a college or pro team
24-hour news	CNN or maybe Fox
Bob Johnson	BET
Petroleum jelly	Vaseline
Vacuum cleaner	Hoover
Tissue	Kleenex
Computer	IBM compatible or possibly Dell
Office supplies	Office Depot or possibly Staples

You may not have a desire for your business product brand or company name to become a household name but, if you want "top dollar" at departure, you must build a certain level of brand recognition or name reputation. Your network of friends, associates, customers, etc., can help you take your company brand or personal brand to tremendous heights.

Take Chrysler, once a company that needed a government bail-out. Since then, it has aligned itself with Mercedes-Benz and improved its image (brand) and perceived value.

For a slightly different take on the normal process of brand awareness, consider your business affiliations. Can they help you take your business to greater heights? As a business owner you want to be careful of the "company you keep" because this will affect your company's bottom line as well as its future potential sales value.

As Valorie Parker, President of Arisebyvnp states, "You should identify public relations experts who understand that their job is to represent the internal or external client better than they do themselves. Look and listen, not just to what they say they can do for you but also what they have actually done for their clients." A public relations professional can help guide you through the process of brand awareness and image enhancement.

GAME PLAN

It is critical to control the marketing tone, the voice, spin, or face you present to outsiders. This tone tells listeners who you are and what type of business you're trying to attract.

If you've ever played sports, you may be familiar with the instruction, "put on your game face," right before a competition. Your coach might have even suggested that a failure to wear your "game face" might tell the opposing team that you are not interested in winning. Look at the proper tone as your voice or game face and take some time to project the image of how you want others to view your company.

FIND YOUR FOCUS

Sometime during the life of a business, your target market or clientele changes. If you can remember back to when you first started or acquired your business, you probably accepted any new clients, even if they did not meet your ideal client profile. Don't worry, this is common among entrepreneurs.

In all likelihood, it didn't take you long to realize that you needed to focus on a particular niche. By working to attract clients that fit a certain criteria, you could make a profit and avoid the added stress of trying to serve a large, diverse population. Unless you have customized services or products, it's better to provide standard packages in order to allow for improvements, value-added pricing, and efficiency.

Examples of niche marketing, illustrating savvy branding opportunities, include:

* AT&T recently announced that it would focus more on business accounts instead of residential customers.

* Large financial institutions are moving back towards private banking and computerizing most other functions. Simulating tellers, banks now have the sophistication to print receipts of cash deposits made via ATM machines.

* Entertainers such as Usher and Russell Simmons have issued their own bank-like "debit" cards, partnering with major virtual partners such as Jackson Hewitt and MasterCard.

* Companies such as Sam's Club and Office Depot are concentrating predominantly on small businesses.

Moreover, many companies are setting up related service lines under one roof. You can see separate brands owned by the same company at strip malls. Sam's Club and Wal-Mart, for example, form a network of stores, branded under separate names, but all dropping profits to the same consolidated bottom line.

BRAINSTORMING IN BRIEF

If you are in need of a marketing plan but want to get some general ideas together before you pay a consultant, consider the following approach:

* Schedule an extended working lunch (three hours should be adequate for now).

* Designate an external or internal facilitator to help keep things flowing and to document all of the ideas.

* Depending on the size of your company, invite the

President, VP Marketing, Director of Operations, and Director of Production.

* If there are many significant divisions or product lines, select additional leaders.

* Try to gather no more than nine people for this preliminary brainstorming meeting. That's the maximum for a productive session.

* Prepare a general agenda that you hand out at the beginning of the session.

* Hold the session offsite. Using your CPA's or your attorney's conference room may keep down the costs. Bring in food but remember that it's a working meeting. (The CPA or attorney is not required to be present for this meeting, which is an operational work session, not a formal board action.)

* Wherever you meet, the space needs to be quiet--no interruptions. Cell phones and beepers must be on vibrate if they can not be turned off completely.

* Have a checklist drafted by your facilitator and sent to the participants, to be returned prior to the meeting. Sample checklist questions include:

  1. What do you do for the company?

  2. Who are your internal and external customers?

  3. What is your personal mantra (the philosophy you live by)? For example, I seek opportunities to meet and network with people who bring additional value to my life. Or, I'm always in search of opportunities to simplify life's challenges or provide resources if I can't personally resolve them.

  4. With which professional organizations are you associated?

  5. Do you hold a position as an officer? If so, which one? Director, Treasurer or President?

  6. What are the three things that most motivate you to do what do you at the office?

During the session the facilitator should provide a warm-up exercise to open up minds to new ideas and get creative juices flowing. One practical example of a warm-up exercise would be for everyone to write down responses, before any group discussion, to the following:

Imagine you have an unlimited budget and can hand-select any team members to create a marketing strategy. What would be the top three areas or divisions that you would start? Why?

VISION TEST

You may get comments indicating a desire for new brochures, an improved Web site, more visible sales representatives at community events, etc. From such answers, you're trying to identify those individuals who have the vision to see past the division in which they currently work.

Additional questions might include:

* Where do you see the company in 10 years, in terms of sales level, new products, etc?

* What are the current overall company objectives and directions, as you see them?

* What are the top three marketing strategies, as you understand them?

The purpose of this session is to allow the facilitator to post responses and assist the team in coming up with a priority list of current perceptions. The next step, as time permits, is to get a few recommendations and priorities for moving forward. You'll also want measurement criteria so you can tell if any of the new marketing strategies are effective.

Remember, this is only the beginning. Nevertheless, if everyone comes ready to work, you will be surprised to discover how far down the road you can develop a marketing plan after meeting for only three hours.

If you use an experienced facilitator you should be able to come up with the beginnings of a formal marketing plan. You also may come away with some tactical strategies and a better idea of where your team feels the company needs to go. This exercise should help you determine if your team members are on the same page as you are. You can judge whether their marketing ideas will lead to the continued growth of your company.

In addition, this exercise allows you to see which team members seem to have vision and innovative strategies. These individuals need to be on your marketing committee.

SUMMARY

A company that works to achieve a high profile within its industry or peer group tends to fare better financially in the short, medium, and long term. Such success also will increase its value as a potential sales target.

Take another look at the chapter, "Begin With the End in Mind--Tuesday Morning: Who is the Customer?" You'll find some additional steps that should be implemented to go along with your marketing plan.

As the leader of your company's management team, it is part of your responsibility to have a clear idea of your market. There are numerous books, courses, Web sites and marketing professionals to provide steps for instructing team members how to develop a practical marketing plan.

Your company's standing in the community, and eventually in the entire country, will be translated into higher returns if you develop a good marketing plan, clearly define your brand or image, and target your desired clientele. The key to any company's success is to know your customer, be able to easily describe your market, and fulfill the needs of that marketplace.

Recommended Books

The Brand Called You, by Peter Montoya

The Origin of Brands, by Al & Laura Ries

Make the Rules or Your Rivals Will, by G. Richard Shell, Jr.

Who Should be on Your Team?

by Genevia Gee Fulbright, CPA

In the late 1990s, when you would hear the word "network," you probably envisioned computers connected together to allow the joint use of printers, software, data files, etc. During the dot-com boom, newly-graduated engineers and information technology (IT) rookies were commanding six-digit salaries and living in the lap of luxury before they wrote their first line of computer code. This was a prime example of great marketing savvy by the tech industry, which created the perception that those workers were "worth their weight in gold"...and it worked for a while.

In this chapter, I am not referring to computer hardware when I refer to a network. Instead, I am talking about the names in your Rolodex, Blackberry, Palm Pilot, or other client contact software. Your professional network (sometimes referred to as center of influence) consists of your friends, associates, referral sources, staff members, vendors, and others who add value to your bottom line, financially or emotionally.

Motivational speaker Les Brown comes to mind when I think about someone who has a strong network of friends and associates who help him create a significant annual cash flow. If you are a professional speaker, Les Brown would certainly be someone you would want on your team of advisors, mentors, investors, strategic alliance partners, etc.

ONE-STOP SHOPPING

To see how networking might pay off, let's take a small event-planning company, with and the owner we'll call Sally. Included in her network are wedding planners, hotels, caterers, florists, event halls, restaurants, a chartered transportation company, and a travel agency.

By providing a one-shop stop, Sally makes it much easier for her customers to take advantage of cost savings she can pass through from strategic network partners. In reality, her associates receive enough business to pass along savings. Moreover, this business is easier for her partners to acquire because all of the marketing dollars normally required to generate new clients are eliminated or at least shared.

In addition, Sally explains the process to potential clients, which eliminates the time others must spend on basic details. A qualified lead, ready to close, is a much easier sale, compared with a prospect who has many details to sort through.

Successful small businesses typically have the following in place:

* Strategic alliances

* Advisory or corporate boards

* A management team, versus only one leader

Remember, if there is a suitor interested in purchasing your business or a new management team scheduled to come on board, the interested parties will want to see that they are moving into a functional operating unit. Re-visit the chapters on "Operations Can Hold Your Company Together" and "Who Should be at the Top?" for additional resources. These chapters provide clarification of leadership requirements and responsibilities as well as prudent operational processes and procedures.

STRATEGY SESSIONS

Maybe you've had a "bad" partnership experience or just want to keep your company small. The wonderful thing about a strategic alliance is that you get to reap some of the benefits of a partnership without taking on the day-to-day involvement or liability exposure of allowing someone else into your business. You can maintain your separate firm and identity while gaining access to a larger potential client base, which should result in higher income.

What is a strategic alliance? It can be an informal or formal agreement between two separate businesses to share costs (such as receptionist's salary, joint advertising expenses, office rent), cross-refer clients, or work on projects jointly at various phases of a contract.

Who should be your strategic alliance partners? That depends on the purpose of your alliance. You might want to expand the services you can offer to your or you may hope to gain access to larger clients.

Using our previous example as a base, let's say you are a caterer who would like to increase your client base. Instead of spending the money, time, and effort to expand into event-planning services, a strategic alliance with a qualified event planner such as Sally can help you attract additional activity and provide expanded services to your clients.

Another example would be a Web site developer who partners with a business attorney, a commercial insurance agent, and others to provide a one-stop shop similar to some of the larger companies. Remember, though, many licensed professionals can not pay referral fees. You might be able to enter into a general agreement that you would get first rights to all potential Web site referrals from all new clients of the other strategic partners.

GREAT MINDS, THINKING ALIKE

Brian "The Sales Doctor" Azar, author of *Your Successful Sales Career*, refers to these strategic alliances as "master mind" groups. He suggests that your group should consist of like-minded professionals who offer complementary services or products. Group members can either work jointly for clients or serve as a referral source to help one another build your businesses and provide needed networking opportunities.

One good way to grow your business into an enterprise that's attractive enough to sell is to form a strategic alliance with a larger, more established company. This allows you to obtain larger contracts, utilize the other company's resources, and gain more exposure to various markets.

As a caution, you should check with your attorney before forming strategic alliances because there might be some potential liability issues. In order to proceed prudently, you should draw up an agreement that spells out the terms of the alliance, specifying who will be responsible for what. You'll want to be clear about the arrangements upfront to avoid confusion, if everything does not work out as planned.

You also must check out the reputation of your strategic alliance partner in the community. If it is a local company, you can ask friends and associates. Your reputation and standing in the community will be affected by the other entity's successful or failed business arrangements.

How do you find strategic partners? Before you start looking, make sure your own house is in order. Specifically, if you are building a positive rapport with your clients, they will be willing to provide referrals and endorsements for your advertisements, Web site, marketing pieces, etc.

Look around your community, if you are locally-based, and nationally, if that's applicable. Find companies that are growing and are considered the best in their markets. If you can find one of the top companies in its industry, that would be ideal. If not, you should look at companies that are considered on the rise and have been gaining market share within their industry.

NINE STEPS TO THE NEXT LEVEL

Here are nine steps to use in forming a productive strategic alliance partnership:

1. Write down your general needs and desires. For example, you might want to expand a particular client base, such as new home owners, by 50% for your lower-end to mid-range furniture store.

2. Identify at least three industries or professions that tend to attract what you need. New home owners might be reached via real estate agents, bridal consultants, and ob/gyn medical practitioners.

3. Write down your marketing strategy. What do you feel you would bring to the table for these potential strategic partners? What would you need from these partners?

Determine stretch goals that go beyond a few referrals. Make sure you answer the "What is in it for me?" question before they ask it.

4. Depending on your company's size and market base (whether it's local, regional, national, or international), identify the top three to four companies in the areas of concentration.

5. Once you narrow down prospective leads for potential strategic partners, meet with them by phone or email so you don't expend a tremendous amount of time on an obvious mismatch. If you're encouraged, meet in person. Find out if they currently have strategic alliances and make sure your competition is not involved.

6. To test out prospective partners, send some of your loyal customers their way, to get feedback. Ask potential alliance partners to test you out as well.

7. If potential partners meet your standards and you are satisfied with how they do business, start to discuss how to formalize the alliance.

8. At this point, get your attorney involved. Have him or her draw up formal agreements.

9. Set up measurement tools and goals in areas such as market penetration, product or firm awareness, etc. Be sure to check against these criteria on a regular basis, looking for additional opportunities.

To find out more about strategic alliances contact your CPA, attorney, banker, commercial insurance broker, Chamber of Commerce, Small Business Center, or other reputable groups specializing in small business consulting.

To form strategic alliances or function as an "incubator" division for a mega-company, prudent corporate governance requires formalized policies and procedures to be in place. Such policies may enable these enterprises to succeed past the infancy or growth stage of development.

ALL A-BOARD

Do you think federal legislation such as Sarbanes-Oxley is the only reason to form advisory or corporate boards? Think again. No matter what happens in Washington, it makes good sense to practice prudent management. Such efforts will comfort outside investors, retired owners with financial ties, top management, and others who have a vested interest in your company's success.

As the owner of a small business, you might not be able to implement all requirements but you should consider trying to implement as much as you can afford. Some financial institutions are starting to look for compliance measures from enterprises that are not publicly-traded companies; such measure may be required for new loans and extensions of credit lines.

Similarly, some venture capitalists require a business to form a board of directors with a seat reserved for one of their representatives, in determining whether to fund a small company. Privately-held small businesses that wish to partner with a larger organization would be well-advised to consider the same strategy.

The more structured and organized you are, the more likely that you can walk away with a lucrative package some day, leaving behind a business that is expected to continue operating smoothly. Therefore, more entrepreneurs are making the momentous decision to establish an advisory board or board of directors.

Think about some of the enterprises that started small and are now successfully employing a significant number of employees. That list goes beyond Apple and Microsoft to include Amazon.com, BET, Black Enterprise, Dell, Federal Express, Gateway, Johnson Publishing, Paychex, Starbucks, Subway, UPS, Yahoo and many others.

Most of these enterprises started out of the garage, basement, or bedroom of the founder's home with a few hundred or a few thousand dollars. Formal boards and other advisors assisted these organizations in taking their enterprises to the next level.

ROLE MODELS

A broad definition of the role of a corporate director is to set policies for a company and to protect the interests of its shareholders (owners). That role is not to manage the operations of the company. Rather, the board acts as a liaison with owners, assists management with the company vision, and looks for opportunities to help the company become more competitive.

Remember, among all of these responsibilities, the main role of the board is to protect the interests of the owners. Therefore, if you own a significant percentage of your company, this board is responsible for protecting your interests--sometimes even protecting you from yourself!

Policies established by the board will help the business create consistent methods for decision-making. Policies related to compensation, accounting, loans, asset acquisitions, and credit can help reduce the principal's liability exposure. Corporate directors also are great sources of capital, market introductions, and overall brand or imaging enhancement.

I often advise businesses owners to consult with board members, especially their external directors, when they are setting up their annual budget and adjusting their marketing plan. It's never too late to do this, particularly if you are trying to improve the structure of your business. The individuals on your board may come from the large organizations forming alliances with your smaller business. Be sure to budget for board fees and expenses--remember that you are using the time of experts and seasoned professionals--but don't break the piggy bank, either.

ADVISE AND CONSENT

If it proves difficult to find individuals willing to associate in a "director" capacity, consider going the advisory board route. Service on an advisory board does not expose the individual members to liability as long as the advisory board does not establish company policies or supervise the owners. (Ask your corporate attorney to establish guidelines that will limit exposure for this volunteer committee). A small per-meeting stipend can be paid to advisory board members.

At large corporations, advisory boards tend to be in a position to monitor key functions. Small-company advisory boards are more likely to provide resources and supervise executive management. Those resources might include introductions to sources of capital and other networking opportunities.

In addition, your company can use its board of directors to help with succession planning advice. An effective board of directors can assist in asking the hard questions that you might avoid, such as, Does John really have the necessary operating skills or should the company look outside the organization to hire a COO?

TEAMING UP

In the chapter entitled, "Who Should be at the Top" Paul Rasmussen emphasizes the importance of having the right individual lead the company. If the right leader is in place, he or she should be able to attract a good management team. This group (which could be as small as three people besides the president) should be able to run the organization if something were to happen to the leader, until another leader is selected.

There are numerous tests designed to determine if individuals have management potential. Read the books listed at the conclusion of this chapter for some additional guidance. Your enterprise will grow and be in a prime position for a successful sale if your management team is in place.

Not long ago, I heard a keynote speaker, Derric A. Gregory, Sr., CPA, a member of the Executive Leadership Council of the National Association of Black Accountants, describe a conversation he had with a recruiter at a top-tier executive search firm. The recruiter described the critical skill sets necessary for leaders within corporate America. I suggest that you look within your current management team to see if you can answer "yes" regarding the individuals on your team, if you are serious about expanding or selling your enterprise:

Is the individual results-oriented? The life blood of an enterprise will be in the timely delivery of products or services to your clients; your company must meet or exceed their expectations consistently. A leader must be able to demonstrate a competitive mindset that sees failure as an unacceptable option; he or she must have the drive and determination to put in the effort necessary for success. True leaders often are able to achieve extraordinary outcomes within fiscal constraints, within the desired time frames, and within the framework of integrity.

Is the individual entrepreneurial? A leader must be willing to employ entrepreneurial thinking if an enterprise is to have long-term viability. He or she must take risks, understanding the rules as well as the context of the game. Entrepreneurial leadership requires remaining focused on how to get results, perhaps thinking "outside the box," without going outside the lines of ethics or integrity. Remember, integrity is not what you do when everyone is around; it's what you do and who you are when no one is looking.

Is the individual a team player? It's not enough to meet budgets and deadlines. Each team member must help other team members accomplish their goals to help the overall team win. Maintaining a competitive mindset is great as long as you help others shine. In order to succeed you must share information freely; you must show up on time, dressed to play, and ready to win. Therefore, you must bring your skills to the table every time. How many times have you met a successful leader who did not have confidence in his or her team? In order to be successful as an entrepreneur, you must be able to assemble a winning team.

Is he or she an excellent communicator? Communication skills (written and oral) are required, particularly verbal. You must have the ability to articulate a vision clearly while conveying the right information to influence and motivate the troops. You must say what you mean and mean what you say.

WACADAD (words are cheap and deeds are dear).

Is the individual a successful networker? You must be able to construct effective relationships with others to get things done. Networking should not be confused with socializing. Rather, it is the strategic art of getting things done through people in a win-win way.

Social capital, the key in both environments, is the intangible that allows one to access the discretionary energy and commitment of another during a time of need, because of previous acts of goodwill. The assist in basketball is a good illustration: there are countless images of James Worthy pointing to Magic Johnson, acknowledging the pass that led to the score. Both are now in the Hall of Fame...that's win-win!!

SUMMARY

Networking and putting together the right team is critical to the growth and subsequent sale of a business. Don't forget old classmates, college professors, relatives, and friends–they all can be great resources for networking and building an effective team.

If you write down your desired management and advisory structure as well as your revenue goals and exit date, you will have a clearer direction. Then you'll be able to work on the strategy you plan to employ to meet your goals. The more detailed you are in describing what you are looking for and how these particular individuals can help you, the easier it will be to get them to assist you.

If you are a business owner on a quest to grow your business, sell it, or leave it as a legacy, you will benefit greatly from all of these teams: a formalized advisory board, a board of directors, strategic alliances, and a quality management team. You'll benefit from innovative ideas generated by seasoned professional and technical leaders, at the modest cost of directors' fees.

Recommended Books

The Entrepreneur's Survival Guide, by Mark Paul

CEO of Self, by Herman Cain

How to Become a Rainmaker, by Jeffrey J. Fox

Funding The Happy Ending

by Genevia Gee Fulbright, CPA

Are you thinking, why would I ever leave the business I spent so many years building? If you have such thoughts, just imagine how nice it would be to take three weeks off in Aruba. Maybe you'd like to visit with friends at their holiday home in Lake Tahoe, skiing for a couple of weeks without bringing along a cell phone or beeper. If such thoughts appeal to you, it's time to start thinking about how to fund the escape or departure from your business.

Perhaps you expect that people will be lined up to purchase your business when you are ready to pack it in. You might hope that your children will take over the enterprise and raise it to levels you only dreamed of achieving during your tenure.

If those are your thoughts...think again!

Strategic planning and workout specialist Dennis Santana of Santana & Associates says, "Many small business owners find that when they are ready to retire, they have very few options to pull out money from their company. As founders build their businesses, they typically reinvest so much of their time, talent, and money that they don't consider that at some point they might be interested in retiring or leaving the enterprise to pursue other goals or investments."

In this chapter, I'll walk you through several viable options of structuring your business so that you can leave your business while it is still healthy. No one wants to be dependent upon others for retirement or daily personal cash flow needs. Your pocket book should remain healthy and you should not have to return to the enterprise to protect your retirement funds.

BOOT CAMP

Most of us bootstrap our business in the beginning and some even continue to do this as we build our enterprises. If you are paying attention to your market and understand your industry, you may eventually build your enterprise to the point where you can make a comfortable living. The question then becomes, "Do you want to continue being the day-to-day operator or can you find a way to fund your "escape?"

In my 20+ years of working with entrepreneurs, I have found that most can be described as having certain styles and mindsets. In essence, there are three different business-owner personality types: the builder, nester, or legacy creator.

BUILDERS: ALWAYS BEGINNING

A builder is a business owner who enjoys starting up companies and operating them for a while. Eventually, a new operations manager needs to get involved to take the business to the next level. Otherwise, the business will perish because this type of owner is more interested in moving on to another project.

A builder is typically open to new ideas and strategies; he or she is good at delegating, strategic planning, and clearly identifying a vision. The ultimate goal, though, is to leave before the organization gets too dependent upon the founder.

Look around your community to see the entrepreneur who is always starting up a new business and combining existing companies, with or without success. Al & Laura Ries, authors of *The Origin of Brands,* suggest that when products or services diverge (become a derivative of or a similar line), there tends to be more success for the company. The computer, for example, has diverged from the mainframe and morphed into a desktop, laptop, and hand-held system with as much memory as some of the original desktops. The business builder, who is very innovative and welcomes a challenge, may be well-equipped to explore different derivatives of an enterprise's original products and services.

However, the builder type of business owner might face a challenge if he or she tries to converge or combine different product lines. Such combinations may work, if they're done for the user's convenience: just look at the pencil you're holding, with its attached eraser.

On the other hand, you don't see significant numbers of individuals purchasing the fax/phone, the Swiss Army knife for the scissors or the screw driver, or combination DVD/VCR player/recorders. Because the builder type is always starting up something new, he or she probably will find more success by sticking with similar business models, products, and services. When you hear of an entrepreneur who starts a car wash business from scratch and then decides to go into the convenience store business two years later, you probably think, what does he know about retail sales?

NESTERS: STAYING PUT

A nester, on the other hand, is a business owner who enjoys hanging around. He or she will continue to operate the business even though others may feel that it's time for a new operations manager to come on board. Whether the business has grown beyond the owner's sophistication level or the owner does not have the vision necessary to go to the next level, a nester has a "job" and wants the business to revolve around him.

This type of owner tends to be a micro-manager. Unfortunately, he might limit his staff to the point where they can't make simple decisions; they must wait for the boss to return or check with him. Nesters are always over-stressed because they fail to delegate tasks and end up having tasks delegated up to the top.

Many nesters neglect succession planning. Therefore, if something happens to the boss, the company is in turmoil because management is very thin and is not accustomed to making decisions. No one has been properly identified as a replacement, to take over the leadership role.

One cautionary example occurred in California, where a

nationally-recognized restaurant thrived. It lasted over 50 years but when the owners died their children were incapable or unwilling to run the enterprise. Consequently, the business ceased operations and the building was sold. This restaurant was a landmark, like so many other home-grown businesses, but failure to establish a succession plan proved to be its downfall.

LEGACY CREATORS: FOCUSING ON THE FUTURE

The legacy creator is a business owner who enjoys building the company to a point where it can live on after his or her departure. This type might even be a second- or third-generation owner. He or she has the vision to take the company to the next level, even if that means bringing in partners or operations managers to run the day-to-day operations. A legacy creator will stay out of the way of progress so the enterprise can reach its true potential.

As is the case with builders, legacy creators are good at delegating yet they stay close enough to the organization to get others to buy into their long-term vision. Those others are motivated to carry on the goodwill built under the legacy creator's tenure. Such individuals tend to think in terms of future generations.

Legacy creators, though, may face a challenge: they might want the business to stay in the family even if there is no member of the next generation interested in running the enterprise. As Jeffrey J. Fox states in his book, *How to Make Big Money in Your Small Business*, in the chapter entitled, "Hire Family--Until the Gene Pool Runs Out," some people don't inherit the "work hard, work smart" gene. He strongly suggests that you encourage family members to take a different path if these individuals are not "genetically wired" to work hard and smart.

Among companies run by legacy creators, the existing staff might not agree with the founder's choice of a successor. If there is a seasoned and loyal staff, legacy creators must make sure that they have planned the departure, put together a compatible team, and communicated with the entire staff.

Legacy creators are typically skilled at delegating so they

might be considered rainmakers, even if they're not responsible for the day-to-day work. An outstanding legacy creator will make sure that everyone in the company is knowledgeable of the history and aware of the future direction of the company. He or she wants the business to live on in perpetuity, which is possible when the company is structured in corporation form.

GOING OUT IN STYLE

No matter where you fit among these alternatives, it is important to understand your personal style so you can realize your strengths, challenges, and limitations. If you have professional advisors, it is important to make them aware of your style. This will make for a team effort, not a tug of war, as these professionals advise you on strategies to fund your escape.

There are numerous options for funding your departure. Primarily, these four alternatives can lead to a smoother transition:

* Hire a business broker to sell your business.
* Bring on a partner and phase out the founder.
* Sell to existing employees.
* Downsize the sale or sell in pieces.

GO FOR A BROKER

Depending on your industry, your trade group might have recommendations, a Web site, or a newsletter that lists potential businesses for sale by owner or through a business broker. By utilizing a business broker, you can position your company to receive qualified prospects as opposed to tire kickers. For this to occur, you must do your homework and find a proven, seasoned broker.

You also can obtain information on the history of sales of your type of business as well as tips based upon the broker's experience. A savvy broker can inform you of how your firm ranks with peers they have sold as well as what's currently on the market for sale. Confidentiality and the ability to be more objective are other benefits of utilizing a broker for the sale.

According to Trip Holmes, a business broker with Sabre Capital, small businesses are typically more difficult to sell because the owner tends to be more intimately involved in the day-to-day operations. Depending on the size of the organization, it might not have an operations manager or mid-level management available to step in after the owner's departure.

Typically, a business broker will need this information:

* Asset listing details (age, current values)
* Financial statements and tax returns for at least the past three years
* Current financial statements
* Owner's description (experience, duties, etc.)
* Management description (experience, duties, etc.)
* Business description and market niche
* Total number of exiting and key employees who are critical or essential to operations
* Timeline of desired sale
* How long the owner is willing to stay during the transition

Yes, a business broker will cost money, but he or she may be able to find a compatible buyer quicker and obtain a better price for your enterprise than you would get on your own.

How does the sale work when dealing with a broker? The broker takes a look at your organization and helps you come up with a possible selling price. Normally, a small fee is charged to put this package together.

The broker then shops the package to potential qualified buyers in his or her network, without disclosing the company's name. Once a qualified buyer comes forward, the negotiations begin. The broker represents the seller in this transaction and should work to maximize the value of the business and obtain the best sales price.

Each business broker is different but typically the broker

will work for a percentage of the sales price. (Some have minimums, such as $15,000). The broker's percentage can range from 5% to 20% depending on the industry, relationship, etc.

How do I get paid in a transaction using a broker? There should be a written agreement that specifies the form of payment and the arrangements to compensate the broker. Some sellers opt to receive all the funds at the date of sale, less the broker's commissions, while others receive a down payment, with the balance due within a specified period of time. The terms are open for negotiation.

In addition, many buyers place a contingency clause in the contract, requiring the selling owner to stick around during a specified transition period. The final sales price might even be based upon such retention factors. Again, if you are going to use a broker, make sure you set the terms before the broker starts qualifying potential buyers and negotiating the sale.

ART OF THE DEAL

Your buyer can seek outside funding, then offer you a cash deal. In some cases, clauses in the contract will call for a down payment while a specified amount is held in escrow. That escrow will be released upon a specified occurrence, such as the collection of receivables or the achievement of a certain sales level.

Another option would call for seller financing of some of the sales price. This is especially likely if the owner plans to stay around with a consulting contract during the transition phase. The terms of the owner financing can vary. An owner might finance 25% or more, especially if the buyer can not obtain full financing or if the company is a service business without much in the way of hard assets.

BANK ON AN INVESTMENT BANKER

You may not desire to provide owner financing when you sell your company. If you wish to make your business holdings more liquid, create more of an incentive to ownership, and transfer assets out of your estate, hiring an investment banker may be another alternative, according to former Wall Street investment banker Aaron Spaulding of Prestige Travel/American Express.

What is the role of an investment banker? The main role of an investment banker is to help a company raise capital, often by underwriting the securities and making a market for them. An investment banker also can provide advice regarding prospective merger and acquisition candidates while handling the media and shareholder relations programs.

Investment bankers assist with debt as well as equity investments. They use valuations specialists as well as other financial experts to assist with the process. In our chapter entitled, "Enhancing Your Company's Value?" Raymond H. H. Dunkle, II, CPA, ABV, CVA, CFE, provides some great guidelines regarding the valuation process.

Although there are no hard and fast rules, the company needs to have at least $2.5 million worth of securities to issue because the typical investment banker's fees start at about 1%, plus expenses. The major national investment bankers usually require an offering of at least $15 million.

How does a sale work when you deal with an investment banker? The investment banker will do all of the detailed financial work for an equity IPO, additional stock offerings, bond issuance, etc. Therefore, before an investment banker will accept your company as a client, you must have the following in place:

* Your story, including a history of how you came into being, where you are now, and where you are going.

* A solid reputation as being a company with integrity, a good place for employees to work, and a positive corporate citizen.

* A history of solid performance, as demonstrated by financial statements that have been reviewed or audited. (For preliminary talks, financials compiled by a reputable CPA firm are acceptable.)

* Long-term viability and profitability, as opposed to

trendiness. Typically, traditional investment bankers do not underwrite trendy companies.

Before you release any of your information to an investment banker you must do your homework. Determine your ultimate goals in terms of how much capital you wish to raise. You also should decide upon the type of investment banker that will be compatible with your company; if you are in a specialized industry, this will narrow the number of firms you can use.

You also must determine who will most likely purchase your stock. Of course, you should also check out an investment banker's references, view its Web site, and go over other materials a firm might provide.

To learn more about investment bankers, visit www.investopedia.com, and www.fortune.com.

PAIR UP WITH A PARTNER

Another approach is to get to know the future owner and operator of your company before you turn over the keys: give your potential successor a test drive. If this appeals to you, consider bringing in a partner and starting to phase your way out of the business.

If you are vital to your company so that your departure will cause the business to decrease in value, you might consider bringing in a financial partner or a junior partner who will gradually take over the daily operations. Think in terms of a famous chef at a restaurant where there is a two-month waiting list for reservations. If patrons find that the chef has moved to another restaurant, they will cease being patrons.

On the other hand, if the famous chef brands his or her cooking style and trains others to perform at the expected level, patrons will continue to dine there. As in any transition, this succession should be planned if you want to avoid a major loss of customers.

Estate Attorney Frances Dyer also reminds us to make

sure to plan for the "3 D's": death, disability and disagreements. Unless you are willing to operate your business with your partner's spouse, always make sure that you have a "buy-sell agreement" in place between the principal business owners, funded by a life insurance policy.

How does the deal work when dealing with a partner buyout? These steps are somewhat tricky. To begin with, you must select a business partner who has a personality compatible with yours, someone whom your existing staff and customers will accept. Goal number one will be to continue to build your business. Remember, this individual is going to take over and you will want to get your money out of the company without disruption.

Initially, your business partner will be worked into the organization. Although your partner can be someone promoted from within, it is more likely that you will choose someone from the outside who has the financing to buy you out eventually. Many founding owners find that it works best if they stay around only during the transition phase, then leave as soon as possible in order to avoid undermining the authority of the new owner when he or she takes over.

How do I get paid in a partner buyout? The new owner can obtain financing to purchase assets or stock in the company. Alternatively, the incoming partner might obtain financing from angel investors or venture capitalists to buy out the existing owner. Sometimes the agreement can include a clause that allows the owner to remain near the business for consulting purposes. Visit my previous book, *Make the Leap: Shift from Corporate Worker to Entrepreneur,* for a chapter entitled, "Don't Start from Scratch, Buy." This chapter, by Joseph Williams, who also contributes to this book, provides some detailed step-by-step tips on how to find and utilize angel investors.

MAKES EMPLOYERS OF YOUR EMPLOYEES

Yet another approach is to sell your company to your existing employees, as a group. This can be done by creating an employee stock ownership plan (ESOP).

Many small businesses have loyal, dedicated employees. "It's like a family working here," says one worker of a small construction company, which is considering selling to an ESOP. "The owner knows my children's names and greets me every morning."

How does the deal work when selling to existing employees? Selling your business to a group of employees is an alternative that should be considered, depending on the industry and the individual company. There are numerous resources at the National Center for Employee Ownership so you should visit its Web site, www.nceo.org, for more information.

Employee ownership allows the staff to control its work environment, play in the entrepreneurial arena on a much larger scale, and become owners of a business where employees have an intimate knowledge. An outside adviser should be consulted to ensure that all the t's are crossed and i's dotted. Some examples of small businesses that are now large businesses after inviting employees to participate in ownership include Whole Foods, Southwest Airlines, and Starbucks,

How do I get paid in a transaction using employee stock ownership? There are many options for privately-held as well as publicly-held companies. If your stock is publicly traded, it is easier to value the shares if the stock is not thinly traded.

With a privately-held company, you would first determine the value of the shares by obtaining a valuation, as explained in the chapter entitled "Enhancing Your Company's Value?" After determining the value, you could do any of the following:

* Offer stock grants to key personnel. When you give stock to these employees, you must report the value as taxable income to the individual recipients.

* Offer stock options to key personnel. This allows the individual to purchase stock, normally at a discount, within a prescribed period of time.

* Sell stock from your personal portfolio of your company's shares. This allows individuals to purchase the shares directly from you; you would have to report taxable

capital gains.

* Issue additional shares and have them purchased by employees, directly from the company. This would allow the company to increase its capital base and cash flow.

A publicly-held company will have more restrictions regarding its stock. If an ESOP does not exist, you might have to go to the shareholders to obtain a majority vote in order to offer such a plan. In addition, there are numerous rules relevant to executive management trading in its own stock that would have to be followed. An SEC attorney would be best suited to handle detailed questions relevant to the specific steps you need to take.

POSITIVE SPIN

If you can't get what you want for the business as a complete unit, spinning off parts of the company might be necessary, according to Dennis Santana. That is, you might sell a division or a department to vendors or competitors. Especially if you're in a niche market, this might be a viable option. Downsizing the sale can work if the buyer does not want the other divisions or is not be able to afford them. With a smaller sale, you can avoid having to offer as much in owner financing.

Large-company examples include AT&T, where the wireless division was a spin-off. More recently, Toys R US spun off Babies R Us. Rifka Rosenwein's Inc Magazine article, "The Spin-Off: Hiding in Plain Sight," mentioned successful spin-offs from Town & Country grill and Identigene, Inc. Although these two companies were connected to the former company, they eventually separated completely and the former company owners have benefited.

How do I get paid in a spin-off deal? There are various ways to get your money out. You might take an equity position in the spin-off company. Alternatively, the spin-off might obtain investors or creditors, allowing new owners to purchase the division from you. Owner financing is another possibility.

FIRE SALE

To conclude this chapter, I'll pass on some excerpts from an interview I recently had with a business owner who successfully sold his small business to a larger enterprise. Dannie Brown of Triangle Fire Extinguisher shared the following advice for any business owner who is interested in selling his or her enterprise:

* Start the process 18-24 months prior to the time when you wish to put your business on the market.

* Get your books in order by making sure that your accounting and tax records are prepared by qualified CPAs. Consider a review or audit.

* Start discussions with a qualified financial advisor such as a CPA and a tax attorney to find out the recommended structure of the sale to minimize tax while helping you maintain cash flow.

* Consider having a valuation performed to see what price range to consider when selling your business.

* Wait for the right buyer.

* Consider selling the business to someone already familiar with your industry because you will most likely get more for your company.

* Have a plan for what you will do in retirement or upon departure. If you plan to consult during the transition phase, have terms drawn up to agree on expectations, goals, etc.

* Make sure you develop your company philosophy in writing prior to engaging the services of a business broker, if you are going to use one.

* Sell your business early in the year to allow adequate time for your CPA or tax attorney to evaluate the tax ramifications of the sale and help you calculate the proper amount of estimated taxes due on the transaction.

Recommended Books

The Art of M&A Financing and Refinancing: Sources and Instruments for Growth, by Alexandra Reed Lajoux and J. Fred Weston

Keep or Sell Your Business: How to Make the Decision Every Private Company Faces, by Mike Cohn with Jayne A. Pearl

Employee Benefits in a Nutshell, by Jay Conison

Enhancing Your Company's Value

by Raymond H. H. Dunkle, II,
CPA, ABV, CVA, CFE

One reason you may want to sell your business is to receive a return on the lifetime you have invested in building a successful company. That intangible value, your "sweat equity," may make your business significantly more valuable than its tangible parts. Quantifying those efforts, though, is an art as well as a science.

Knowing how valuations are established can help you increase your company's worth to a potential buyer. The same knowledge, moreover, can help you avoid the biggest mistake business owners make when selling their business: relying on a "rule of thumb" to determine a value.

COMING TO TERMS

Believe it or not, the term "value" means different things to different people in the world of business valuation. The value of a business to an individual investor may be extremely different from the value of that same business to a competitor. Therefore, you need to know what "value" can mean.

While there are many different definitions of value, we are going to concentrate on the two that you are most likely to encounter in selling a small business: fair market value and investment value.

Fair market value is defined as "the price, expressed in terms of cash equivalents, at which property would change hands between a hypothetical willing and able buyer and a hypothetical willing and able seller. It is assumed that the buyer and seller are acting at arm's length in an open and unrestricted market, when neither is under compulsion to buy or sell and when both have a reasonable knowledge of the relevant facts."

A key factor to this definition is the concept of hypothetical buyers and sellers: individuals who do not have special motivations influencing their determination of value. This is typically the standard of value in an arm's length transaction where buyers and sellers have the ability and willingness to complete a transaction.

Investment value is defined as "the value to a particular investor based on individual investment requirements and expectations." This measure of value varies dramatically from fair market value because it is affected by the buyer's personal interests. To drive home the differences in these standards, let's study a simple example.

COMPETITIVE EDGE

Imagine that you own a small business specializing in the production of high-quality plastic buckets and that you control the Ohio market. You have decided to sell your business and retire to Florida. You have been approached by two interested buyers: (1) a young MBA who managed to retain some wealth from the dot-com craze; and (2) your biggest competitor, who controls the plastic bucket market in every state east of the Mississippi, except for Ohio.

The young MBA is most likely looking at fair market value--he needs your sales force, your back office functions, your production facilities, etc. Therefore, he also needs to incur all the costs that come with establishing a business. He wants to own a business and, no matter what industry he enters, he needs to acquire the proper business foundations, which will come at a cost.

Now, consider your competitor. He already has functioning plants, back office functions, and an established sales force. With relatively little effort, he can acquire your customer base, eliminate many of your costs and finally tie up the one elusive state that he has not been able to dominate.

Who's going to pay more? Your competitor, most likely. He'll be willing to pay more because your business has a special investment value. Acquiring your company will give him the market he wants while earning net income greater than you were able to produce. (Remember, he can eliminate many of your expenses.)

It is important to keep in mind, however, that an interested competitor is not required to pay an investment value. In fact, it is in his interest to pay the lower fair market value.

As S. Todd Burchett, CPA, ABV, a business valuation consultant with The Hanke Group in San Antonio, Texas, says, "There is no law that a strategic buyer must pay an investment value. However, part of my job is to help sellers recognize how much money they may be leaving on the table if they sell for fair market value. Business owners are frequently satisfied selling for fair market value but they should be careful not to sell themselves short by not considering buyer motivations."

RUNNING OR RUN-DOWN?

Another concept that you should recognize when you're planning to sell your business is that of "premise of value." Generally speaking, a business is going to be sold on a "going concern" premise or a "liquidation" premise.

Going concern premise is the value for a business that is functioning, with its income-producing assets in place. This premise applies when individuals purchase an operating business.

Liquidation premise applies to assets that are no longer producing income. They may be sold, together or individually, to an interested party who will use such assets for his or her own purposes.

Which premise is appropriate? Because this book deals with selling your business, this discussion assumes that you are selling a controlling interest in your business. Usually, in valuing a controlling interest, the business valuer must determine the "highest and best use" of the company's assets.

In determining the highest and best use, the valuer must consider the cash flow generated by the business as well as the value of its tangible assets and liabilities.

MASTERING THE MENU

To give a simple example of how these factors affect the value of your business, let's consider the case of a small restaurant. The restaurant's primary assets (assuming the building is leased) include its kitchen equipment and dining furniture, which are worth $100,000, and the restaurant has no liabilities.

Assume that for each of the last five years, the restaurant had a profit of $1,500 per year. Further assume that the owner was paid $20,000 per year, for working 80 hours per week.

The owner has now decided to sell the business. Under which approach is the owner going to receive the greatest amount of cash: selling the equipment for $100,000 (liquidation) or selling the business as a going concern? You do not need to be a business valuation expert to conclude that one would not pay more than $100,000 to work 80 hours per week, and assume the headaches of ownership, just to earn $21,500 per year.

If all the facts were the same except that the owner worked 50 hours per week, earned $80,000 per year and received an additional profit of $50,000 per year, our conclusion likely would be that the going concern approach has greater value.

THUMB'S DOWN

As mentioned, estimating the value of your business by using a rule of thumb can be a costly error. Your life's work is far too important to sell without adequately considering the many important factors that can impact the value of your business.

What are those factors? The Internal Revenue Service's Revenue Ruling 59-60 does an excellent job of identifying key factors. Revenue Ruling 59-60 notes the following:

* The nature of the business and the history of the enterprise from its inception.

* The economic outlook in general as well as the condition

and outlook of the specific industry in particular.

* The book value of the stock and the financial condition of the business.

* The earnings capacity of the company.

* The company's dividend-paying capacity.

* Whether or not the enterprise has goodwill or other intangible value.

* Sales of the stock and the size of the block of stock to be valued.

* The market price of stocks of corporations engaged in the same or similar line of business having their stocks actively traded in a free and open market, either on an exchange or over the counter.

Each of these factors can have significant impact on the value of your business. Is the business new and unknown, or is it established with a dedicated core of customers? Is the company in a rapidly growing industry, or one that is quickly dying off? Is the company financially superior to its competitors, or is it merely keeping pace with the herd? Are investors uninterested in companies of this type or are they paying a premium to have ownership in them?

The answers to these questions may have dramatic impacts on value. Without thorough financial analysis (that is, by using a rule-of-thumb approach), it is very easy to misstate the value of your business.

BALANCING ACT

Generally speaking, three approaches to business valuation should be considered on every company being valued: the asset approach, the income approach, and the market approach.

The *asset approach* is defined as "a general way of determining a value indication of a business, business ownership interest, or security by using one or more methods based on the value of the assets of that business net of liabilities." More simply stated, this approach adjusts the company's assets and liabilities to their fair market value and estimates the value of the business as the net of the two.

To see this method in action, let's refine our hypothetical restaurant example, described above. Assume that Billy Bob of Billy Bob's House of Hamburgs has decided to retire. Billy Bob wants to know the value of his business under an asset approach. Currently, Billy Bob's balance sheet looks like this:

Cash		$1,000
Equipment (net)	20,000	
Building(net)	300,000	
Total Fixed Assets		320,000
Total Assets		$321,000
Accounts Payable		$121,000
Equity		200,000
Total Liabilities & Equity		$321,000

Without making adjustments, one would conclude that, under an asset approach, the value of Billy Bob's is $200,000 ($321,000 in assets less $121,000 in liabilities).

Now let's assume that two new pieces of information have come to our attention. First, the appraised value of the building is $560,000 ($260,000 more than on the balance sheet). Second, Billy Bob did a poor job of maintaining his equipment and it is really worth only $10,000 (one-half of what is reported on the balance sheet).

As a result of these findings, or "fair market value" adjustments, we have identified a net addition to value of $250,000. Under an asset approach, Billy Bob's is worth $450,000 ($200,000 plus $250,000).

Keep in mind that this scenario, like all the examples in this chapter, is over-simplified. Nevertheless, such straightforward examples are useful for clarifying key points.

COUNTING ON CASH FLOW

The *income approach* is far more complicated than the asset approach. It is defined as "a general way of determining a value indication of a business, business ownership interest, security, or intangible asset using one or more methods that convert anticipated benefits into a present single amount."

Under this approach, the appraiser attempts to estimate the value of a business, based on anticipated future cash flows. To do this, valuers must accomplish two difficult tasks:

1.   Identify an appropriately "normalized" cash flow stream; and

2.   Identify an appropriate "capitalization" or "discount" rate.

When we refer to a "normalized" cash flow stream, we mean a level of cash flows that the new business owner can reasonably expect to enjoy. For example, let's say that Billy Bob's cash flows were $50,000 in 2004, $100,000 in 2003 and $10,000 in 2002. These amounts are all over the board, making it difficult to determine what amount of cash flow the value of the business should be based on.

Let us say, however, that upon further investigation we learned that in 2003, Billy Bob received a bonus of $50,000 for selling a winning lottery ticket (in the now cancelled state Lotto). In 2002, Billy Bob had to spend $40,000 repairing his building, due to flood damage.

Remove the $50,000 from 2003 that Billy Bob will never again earn, and add back the $40,000 to 2002 that Billy Bob will not likely again incur, and the cash flows become comparable, $50,000 each year.

FLOW CHARTING

The "capitalization" or "discount" rate is akin to the multiple that we must apply to cash flows to determine the value of the business. To determine this number, we must consider the rates of return available for other investments.

As a business owner, you are very well aware of the concept of risk vs. return. In determining the capitalization or discount rate, we are attempting to identify the appropriate return one should earn for taking on the risk of buying your business. Typically, we do this through what's referred to as the "build-up" method.

With this approach, we begin with a risk-free rate (from a 20-year U.S. Treasury bill) and build up to a rate of return one would expect to earn on an investment in a particular business. This build-up considers risk-free investments, investments in equities, particular industry characteristics, characteristics specific to the company, and the company's expected growth rate.

Once we know this rate, we typically also consider the going cost of debt (interest rates) and estimate the portion of a business that can be financed with debt, versus the portion that must be funded with equity (i.e., direct cash outlays by the investor) in order to determine the weighted average cost of capital (WACC), which becomes our value multiplier.

Going back to Billy Bob's, our normalized cash flow was $50,000. Now assume we determined a WACC of 10%. This 10% WACC equates to a ten times multiplier (100% divided by 10% equals 10). Our estimate of value for Billy Bob's becomes $50,000 times ten or $500,000.

COMPARABLE CALCULATIONS

The *market approach* is conceptually familiar to most people. It is defined as "a general way of determining a value indication of a business, business ownership interest, security, or intangible asset by using one or more methods that compare the subject to similar businesses, business ownership interests, securities, or intangible assets that have been sold."

Under this approach, the valuer attempts to determine value by considering transactions involving similar businesses, much like a real estate appraiser estimates the value of a home based on sales of similar homes. To apply this approach, the business valuer analyzes prices of similar, publicly-traded companies as well as the amounts paid for merged or acquired companies.

A market approach requires access to business transaction databases and requires thoughtful consideration to ensure benchmarked companies are reasonably comparable to the entity under valuation. This includes considering the capital structure, credit status, nature of competition, products, management, earnings capacity, and numerous other factors.

Once comparable companies are identified, the valuer must determine appropriate valuation multiples using them, and must determine that the selected valuation multiples are statistically valid. Possible valuation multiples are extensive but can include price/earnings, price/revenues, price/book value, and price/EBITDA (earnings before interest, tax, depreciation and amortization).

THREE FOR THE MONEY

Let's return to Billy Bob's. Assume that using the market approach, the valuer determined that a price/EBITDA multiple of 3.0:1 is statistically valid for companies such as Billy Bob's. Now assume that Billy Bob's EBITDA was $183,333.33. Using the 3.0 multiple, and assuming that no additional adjustments are warranted, we would conclude on a value of $550,000 ($183,333.33 x 3.0).

After completing the various valuation approaches, the valuer considers the applicability of each, weights them, and concludes on a value. In our scenario, we have estimated values of $450,000, $500,000 and $550,000, from the three different methods. Assuming equal weighting, we would conclude on a value of $500,000, which is the average of the three approaches. This value may be subject to the discounts noted below.

DEALING IN DISCOUNTS

Businesses can be subject to various premiums and discounts. The two most commonly experienced are a discount for lack of control, which is applied when a shareholder does not own a controlling interest, and a discount for lack of marketability, which recognizes that purchasers of business interests, which are not readily marketable, will demand a discounted share price as an enticement to taking an ownership interest.

In each case, these discounts are determined based on specific characteristics of the company and are estimated using objective studies. The range of possible discounts is quite broad and such discounts may have a significant impact on value.

Picking up the example of Billy Bob's, assume we are selling only a 10% interest in the company. Also assume we have determined that a discount for lack of control of 25% is applicable and a discount for lack of marketability of 20% is applicable. Our estimated value would be as follows:

Estimated value	$500,000	
10% interest	x 10%	= 50,000
Less: 25% (lack of control)		(12,500)
		37,500
Less: 20% (lack of marketability)		(7,500)
		$30,000

As you can see, discounts can significantly reduce the entity's value.

ON THE PATH TO PROFITS

In performing valuation work, I am often asked, "How do I increase the value of my business?" As business valuator Michael A. Longobardo, CPA, ABV, CVA, DABFA of Penny, Longobardo & Company, P.A., of Raleigh, North Carolina, who performs an extensive amount of merger and acquisition work, says, "There is no magic bullet for increasing value. Business owners cannot decide one day to sell their business and expect some sort of accounting sleight-of-hand to lead to untold riches. Owners must plan with the end in mind, many years in advance of selling, if they expect to redeem a maximum value from their business."

This explanation mirrors my own belief. Unless you are fortunate enough to be in a "hot" industry where buyers are paying large premiums, there is no substitute for profitability.

To enhance value, therefore, business owners must pursue a path of profit improvement. This can mean many things:

* Benchmarking financial performance to the industry, and outperforming the industry.

* Benchmarking compensation to ensure reasonable, but not excessive, employee compensation.

* A policy of perpetually streamlining operations, improving productivity, and reducing expenses.

* Training employees. (Is it riskier to train employees with the possibility that they will leave, or not train them only to have them stay?!)

* Consistently being innovative, by providing products and services that remain relevant.

* Releasing the reins--remembering that even the most successful business owner can lose touch with the current market.

Finally, I strongly suggest that business owners avoid the temptation to use a rule of thumb to value their business. These rules of thumb are frequently without merit and cannot properly consider the complexities of business valuations or the specifics of a given transaction.

For instance, a rule of thumb for a tow truck business is that value equals a multiple of revenues plus fixed assets. Would you be happy to learn that you sold your highly profitable, debt-free business for the same price as your unprofitable, debt-laden competitor, just because you had the same annual revenues and fixed asset balances? The cost of a proper business valuation can easily be substantially less than the mistake of not having one.

SUMMARY

Selling a business can be an emotional undertaking but a

company's value can not be determined emotionally. The proper valuation contexts must be considered, including the buyer's motivations and the seller's financial performance. Several valuation approaches should be evaluated and empirical data, not rules of thumb, should be relied upon.

Business owners also must recognize that selling non-controlling interests in their business can lead to substantial reductions in value because of applicable discounts. Further, there are no magic bullets--increasing the value of a business often takes time, proactive planning, and increased profitability. With this knowledge, you are armed with the information needed to intelligently ensure that your sweat equity is being properly valued!

Recommended Books

Financial Valuation - Applications and Models, by James R. Hitchner. Published by John Wiley & Sons, Inc.

Business Valuation Discounts and Premiums, by Shannon P. Pratt. Published by John Wiley & Sons, Inc.

Valuing Small Businesses & Professional Practices, by Shannon P. Pratt, Robert F. Reilly and Robert P. Schweihs. Published by McGraw-Hill.

Recommended Web Sites

www.bvmarketdata.com. You'll find a variety of databases offering financial and transactional data relating to the sales of public and privately held companies, control premiums, minority discounts, and marketability discounts.

www.firstresearch.com. This site provides in-depth, industry-specific research.

www.erieri.com. Here, you have access to compensation studies specific to job title, industry, geographic region, and company size.

Does Money = Success?
A Perfect Life Attracts the Right Opportunities

by Genevia Gee Fulbright, CPA

Do you ever have disagreements about money with your family or business partner? I regularly consult with entrepreneurs who express concerns over having a different "money philosophy" than the people around them.

You might ask, what is a money philosophy? It's your concept of the purpose of money and how you think it should be used. Some people actually perceive money as evil, as a means of exercising power over others. For further ideas on money, get a copy of *Facing Financial Dysfunction*, by Bert Whitehead, MBA, JD, at your local bookstore.

I recall working with an entrepreneur who had problems treating his finances realistically. His company was having cash flow problems. Rationally, he should have sold his excess business vehicles while reducing his expenses by cutting back on golf and ski trips. He could have switched to a more cost-effective cell phone service and stopped dining in expensive restaurants.

Instead, he continued to spend money as if his business was generating a significant profit. You know the "rest of the story": this individual eventually lost his business and had to sell his investment properties at fire-sale prices.

MONEY IS A TOOL

In my opinion, money is a tool to be used to invest in the type of lifestyle you wish to enjoy, now and in the future, for yourself and perhaps a surviving spouse. You can use your money to share with others who are less fortunate. If you wind up with more money than you need, for those purposes, you can leave a legacy for future generations.

Among the available options for generating money, my life choice is to be self-employed. Having your own business can be a wonderful adventure. Alternatively, it can be an excruciating journey if you do not have:

* A marketing plan

* Quality staff

* Quality equipment

* Qualified professional advisors

* A retirement plan

* An exit strategy

Throughout this book, we have introduced various ways you can improve operations and enhance the value of your business.

CREATE A PERFECT LIFE

The other day, while chatting with a colleague, he mentioned that he felt he was living the perfect life. My first response was, Wow! Do I know any others who can honestly say they have a perfect life?

Then, of course, my analytical side kicked in and I started to think of people who might be perceived as living the perfect life. I conducted a quick, non-scientific survey to define the term "perfect life" and prepare a checklist for those of us who have not yet achieved this goal.

When I started to discuss this concept with associates, I thought that the way to attract the perfect life, or at least be able to afford it, was to look at ways to maximize your income and returns on your investments. Yes, please understand this is a very important ingredient to the "perfect life" formula but, as one of my clients advised me, money is not the only ingredient. It takes more than cash to motivate you to get up every morning and excite you to go into the office, then spend two-thirds of your waking hours with individuals other than your loved ones.

Therefore, after talking to several colleagues and clients, I came up with a definition of what constitutes a perfect life. First, you need a balance between all of the following:

* Adequate time for family and friends

* Exciting hobbies, travel opportunities, and entertainment

* Finances in the proper perspective: adequate cash flow and investments to meet your desired lifestyle

* Spiritual house in order and a knowledge of what you were placed here on earth to accomplish

* Successful career: advancements or entrepreneurial acquisitions meeting expectations

* Time for big dreams and energy for dream implementation

VISUALIZE YOUR GOAL

Next, you must devise a way to achieve this goal. Listed below are some action items that might be useful in the process:

* Visualize what a perfect life looks like.

* Determine what it will take financially, emotionally, and physically to achieve the life you visualize.

* Determine the risks of attempting to meet your goals.

* Determine if you are willing to take the risks. Is it worth it?

* Determine who is on your team: friends, family, coaches, consultants, etc.

CALL FOR A COACH

There are actually financial and life coaches who help their clients achieve certain degrees of the perfect life. For a number of checklist resources, tools, and referrals visit the International Coach Federation at www.internationalcoachfederation.com.

I personally have not created the perfect life yet, but I am working on it. According to my associate, everyone should try to achieve it because it's wonderful to be in the position of enjoying life, feeling that you are living out your dreams and fulfilling your life purpose.

SHARE INTELLECTUAL AND ECONOMIC RESOURCES

During a recent national convention, I met numerous delegates from South Africa including Jeff van Rooyen, Founding Member of the Advancement of Black Accountants in Southern Africa (ABASA) and currently the Executive Officer of the Financial Services Board (similar to the U.S. Securities Exchange Commission). A historic signing of a memorandum of understanding took place between two groups, the National Association of Black Accountants' (NABA's) Division of Firms and ABASA, confirming plans to leverage intellectual capital. This will include staffing exchanges, continuing professional education, business development, and economic as well as cultural empowerment.

During my interview with Mr. van Rooyen, he emphasized that everyone benefits when all companies are financially stable and able to compete. He believes that a competitive playing field helps the financial markets to benefit the investing public.

What are you doing to share your intellectual capital and economic resources? I contacted a few associates to help come up with a list of some organizations that were creating opportunities for business and professional citizen stakeholders. Although this does not represent an all-inclusive list, you will find some helpful resources:

* Chamber of Commerce (search for your local area), www.uschamber.com

* Department of Commerce, www.commerce.gov

* NABA Division of Firms, www.nabadof.org

- * National Association of Corporate Directors, www.nacdonline.org

- * National Federation of Independent Business, www.nfib.com

- * Office of Small Business Development Centers, www.sba.gov/sbdc

- * Small Business Administration (SBA) and Service Corps of Retired Executives (SCORE), www.sba.gov

Start with the Web sites above to locate training resources and contacts for increasing your intellectual and economic resources. In addition, most states have college systems that house business centers. If you are in the position to share your resources, consider volunteering or supporting one of these groups. This is a wonderful way to network.

IT IS UP TO US

The President of ABASA, Futhi Mtoba, says that her country has a saying, "if it has to be, it is up to us." I think this theme gives all of us a charge. We should take the time to share our intellectual capital, spend more time utilizing the educational resources in our area. and leverage opportunities to increase our collective wealth.

Recommended Books

Live Your Dreams, by Les Brown

The Traveler's Gift: Seven Decisions that Determine Personal Success, by Andy Andrews

Listen to Your Life, by Valorie Burton

Coaching by the Book, by Ruth Ledesma

What About my Business?

In Conclusion, by Genevia Gee Fulbright

Being a business owner is exhilarating, challenging, and rewarding. I remind my clients constantly to always remember to have fun and keep dreaming up ways to make your business more exciting. As Michael Shinn, CFP, said recently while running a workshop where I was a guest panelist, "DO SOMETHING!"

This book was written to provide some practical tips you can implement immediately to re-position your company. These tips can help you get the best team in place, create the ideal operating structure, and seek alternatives for departing.

We've explored looking beyond yourself, if you don't happen to have a management team at your disposal, and we've even discussed whether or not the current owner is always the right owner. Building a team--whether it's internal, external or some combination--allows you to expand your company and position it for the right opportunity, allowing for a smooth ownership transition.

If after reading this book and following up on the Web sites as well as the book suggestions, you need help finding an advisor or just have a question you need answered don't hesitate to send me an e-mail. Contact me at ggf@moneyful.com and we'll see if we can direct someone to help you or provide a resource.

About the Author

Genevia Gee Fulbright, CPA

Genevia is currently the Vice President and Marketing Director of Fulbright & Fulbright, CPA, PA, a tax, financial consulting, and coaching company that concentrates on creative, licensed, and technical professionals as well as entrepreneurs, retirees, and educators.

Professional accomplishments include:

- Certified Public Accountant
- Author of several books
- Columnist for local and national magazines
- Corporate director for a publicly-traded company
- Senior Financial Advisor for a national accounting group
- Project manager, casting director, and actor for a corporate director video
- Leader of a team that hosted a financially successful local Chamber of Commerce event
- Consultant that helped formalize board communications and protocol for a non-profit organization

Selected national and regional media and publishing credits:

- CNBC
- NBC17
- BET.com
- Black Enterprise
- Director's Monthly

- Ebony
- Fortune Small Business
- Heart & Soul
- Journal of Accountancy
- NewsPlus
- NPR Affiliate WNCU, "Mastering Your Money"
- NiaOnline
- Oakland Tribune
- Parade Magazine
- Spectrum
- Tax Hotline
- The Bev Smith Show
- Triangle Business Journal
- UNC TV, Black Issues Forum
- Working Woman

Motto she lives by:

Always in search of opportunities to help others achieve greatness!

Contact information:

Genevia Gee Fulbright, CPA
Vice President/Marketing Director
Fulbright & Fulbright, CPA, PA
Post Office Box 13156
Research Triangle Park, NC 27709-3156
www.moneyful.com
www.makeleap.com
(919)544-0398

About the Chapter Contributors

Walter Turek

Chapter: Foreword

- Current role: Senior Vice President of Sales and Marketing for Paychex, Inc., a Fortune 500 company that concentrates on employer administrative and human relations services and products.
- Best described by friends and co-workers as: An inspirational leader in building world class sales organizations.
- Three most exciting professional milestones:
  * Growth of start-up company to billion-dollar-plus organization
  * 500,000 clients, adding over 100,000 new clients a year
  * International expansion
- Greatest contribution: Creating an environment for motivated individuals to maximize personal potential
- Contact Information: www.paychex.com
- Phone: (800) 828-4411

Linda Poulson, Ph.D., CPA

Chapter: Preface

- Current role: Associate Professor of Accounting in the Love School of Business at Elon University in North Carolina.
- Best described by friends and co-workers as: Someone who models the phrase by Richard Henry Dann, "He who dares to teach must never cease to learn."
- Three most exciting professional milestones:
  * Becoming a tenured professor
  * Becoming a CPA and obtaining a Ph.D.
  * Becoming a manager in a Big Four accounting firm

- Greatest contribution: Serving as a tutor and mentor for the Saturday Academy program. The Saturday Academy, a school-based academic enrichment program, helps students acquire the academic skills and character traits necessary to succeed in the classroom and the community.

- Contact information: www.elon.edu

- e-mail: poulson@elon.edu

- Phone: (336) 278-5923

Joseph "J.W." Williams

Chapter: Begin with the End in Mind: Tuesday morning -- Who is the Customer?

- Current role: President of Staircase and Millwork Corporation (dba Mr. Stair), a multi-million-dollar staircase enterprise; Co-Founder and Principal of The Wakefield James Management Group, LLC, a private investment firm.

- Best described by friends and co-workers as: A high energy deal maker, salesman, and networker

- Three most exciting professional milestones:

    * Before turning 30 (and fresh out of business school) started an investment firm by raising $485,000 for a blind pool.

    * At 31 years old, purchased a multi-million-dollar business via bank debt, seller paper, and investor equity

    * Studied overseas in Japan, became very proficient in Japanese, and secured a position as the only American employee in Japan for a major Japanese company

- Greatest contribution: Assisted a person of moderate means reach an Ivy League college through personal coaching, mentoring, and providing financial assistance

- Contact information: www.wakefieldjames.com and www.mrstair.com

- e-mail: jwilliams@wakefieldjames.com

- Phone: (404) 217-3968

Paul Rasmussen

Chapter: Who Should be at the Top?

- Current role: President of Tyson Street Partners, a mergers/acquisitions consulting practice and venture capital firm

- Best described by friends and co-workers as: A serial entrepreneur

- Three most exciting professional milestones:

    * Starting and selling my first company

    * Advising one of my sons while he starts his first company

    * Preparing two businesses to go public

- Greatest contribution: Being involved in building successful companies that create value to all stakeholders (investors, employees, customers, and the community) and successfully selling or playing a significant role in the sale of over 25 companies

- Contact information: www.tysonstreet.com

- e-mail: paul@tysonstreet.com

Deborah A. Cowan, CPA

Chapter: Operations Can Hold Your Company Together

- Current role: Vice President of Finance for Radio One , Inc., the seventh largest radio broadcasting company in the United States, and the largest radio broadcasting company in the United States primarily targeting African-Americans. She is responsible for planning, budgets, forecasting, and measurements while serving as Project Leader for the company's Sarbanes-Oxley 404 compliance effort.

- Best described by friends and co-workers as: A consummate financial professional and subject matter expert in the arena of corporate financial operations.

- Three most exciting professional milestones:

- * Becoming a CPA
- * Serving on a number of non-profit boards that contribute to society
- * Obtaining diverse finance experience
- – Contact information: www.radio-one.com
- – email: dcowan@radio-one.com

Raymond H. H. Dunkle, II, CPA, ABV, CVA, CFE

Chapter: Enhancing Your Company's Value

- – Current role: Senior Manager, Litigation, Valuation & Forensic Services and Accounting & Advisory Services Groups, Bober, Markey, Fedorovich & Company, a full-service CPA consulting firm
- – Best described by friends and co-workers as: A creative thinker with a strong work ethic focused on providing high-quality, responsive client service. A family man.
- – Three most exciting professional milestones:
  - * Publishing and contributing to numerous articles in specialty valuation niche
  - * Testifying at the Supreme Court of Ohio
  - * Obtaining four professional designations, each on the first attempt
- – Greatest contribution: Actively serving on the board of numerous non-profits that serve families in crisis and individuals in need, such as The American Red Cross, Child Guidance and Family Solutions, and The Healthy Connections Network.
- – Contact information: www.bobermarkey.com
- – e-mail: rayd@bobermarkey.com
- – Phone: (330) 255-2455

Acknowledgments

The "Make the Leap" book series grew out of a conversation I had with my former literary agent, Susan Barry, who helped secure my first contract, for three e-books, several years ago. At the time, I mentioned to her that I wanted to write a book series and inquired how to become a best-selling author in today's environment. It was through her and the encouragement of others that I decided to venture out and tackle the exciting journey of writing a book series.

This book, *Make the Leap: From Mom & Pop to Good Enough to Sell*, has been written with the input of many friends, associates, and family members. It would take an entire book to name all the people who assisted so I will take the liberty of acknowledging some of the people below who were not individually quoted in the book and listing some of my organizations. Everyone listed below either supported me in person or in spirit throughout the project:

- Ed, my husband, a holistic and comprehensive financial planner, host of the syndicated finance radio talk show, "Mastering Your Money."

- Cammy, my sweet daughter who is an avid reader, soon-to-be proficient bass guitarist, "pretend" game show host, and one of my best sales associates

- My parents and my in-laws, all happy early retirees

- Grandmother Mamoo, who always reminded me to set goals

- Paternal Grandfather and Maternal Great-Grandmother (both deceased), from whom I inherited the entrepreneurial genes

- The clients and staff of both Fulbright & Fulbright, CPA, PA and Fulbright Financial Consulting, PA

- Sisters-in-law, Gina and Michelle

- Brother and brother-in-law, Rip and Chris

- Favorite teacher, Erma J. Owens (deceased)

- Relatives, living and deceased, who continue to provide inspiration

- Oakland Running Crew: Ana, Antoinette, Carmen, Catherine, Celeste, Corinne, Edith, Elaine, Henry, Jeff, Jetty, Michael, Ron, Sandra, Tyra, Veronica, Zella, and Zina

- Editor: Donald Jay Korn

- Foreword contributor: Walter Turek

- Preface contributor: Linda Poulson, Ph.D., CPA

- Chapter contributors: Deborah Cowan, CPA; Raymond H. H. Dunkle, II, CPA, ABV, CVA, CFE; Paul Rasmussen; and Joseph "J.W." Williams

- Cover designer: Jay Dubard of Envisual, Inc.

- Media Coach: Willis Smith of W.G. Smith & Associates

- Print Media Coach: Edwin Moss of the Pride of Durham

- Sales Coach: Brian "The Sales Doctor" Azar of The Sales Catalyst

- Travel Booking Agent: Aaron Spaulding of Prestige Travel

- Hair Quarters friends, who populate the best spot for quiet pondering and writing

- Armando G. Roman, CPA, previous book partner

- AICPA, NABA, NBMBAA, NCACPA, and SBTDC friends

- Tom Joyner Cruise friends